GOD ISN'T FINISHED
WITH US YET

GOD ISN'T FINISHED WITH US YET

Major Promises from the Minor Prophets

James A. Harnish

Cover design: Steve Laughbaum
First printing: August, 1991 (5)
Second printing: August, 1992 (5)
ISBN 0-8358-0644-8
Library of Congress Catalog Card Number: 91-65723

Printed in the United States of America

WITH GRATITUDE
for the prophetic witness
of the people and staff
of
Central Methodist Mission,
Johannesburg,
South Africa

". . . enduring the suffering
that comes to those who belong to his kingdom."
Revelation 1:9

: CONTENTS :

INTRODUCTION

THEY ARE THE "MAYTAG REPAIRMEN" OF SCRIPTURE. Like the repairmen in the television commercials who spend lonely hours in offices where the telephones never ring, the Minor Prophets of Israel are tucked away in the closing pages of the Old Testament. They are unknown and unused by folks who simply can't imagine any good reason to need them. They are the least-read, least-quoted, least-known characters in scripture.

Church historian Martin Marty confessed that his Old Testament professor hurried through the minor prophets so quickly that he dropped a pencil and while picking it up missed Nahum, Habakkuk, and Zephaniah.

We have several reasons to avoid them. They have been given very bad press. For some of us, the word *prophet* conjures up the image of nasty, little men in long, dreary robes whose full-time occupation is finding people who are having fun and telling them to stop. We see them as gloomy, old coots who get their kicks out of raining down wrath on everyone else's parade, as depressing purveyors of judgment and doom. We picture them the way John Steinbeck described Liza Hamilton in *East of Eden:*

> A tight hard little woman humorless as a chicken. She had
> a. . . code of morals that pinned down and beat the brains
> out of nearly everything that was pleasant to do. . . .She was
> suspicious of fun whether it involved dancing or singing or
> even laughter. She felt that people having a good time were
> wide open to the devil.

It doesn't help that these prophets have such intimidating names. Scanning the table of contents is enough to frighten most readers away. To complicate matters further, their prophecies are set against the backdrop of ancient political and social structures that are foreign to our contemporary culture. At first they seem light years removed from people or places to which we can relate.

There is another little piece of information that adds confusion and misunderstanding to our study of the prophets. While most of the minor prophets are historically verifiable figures, a few of these books are the result of oral tradition, such as Jonah, or the work of more than one writer, such as Zechariah. While acknowledging these textual concerns, we can still hear the prophetic word that has been handed down to us in this form.

The final stroke is the title "minor prophets," which sounds a good deal like the "minor leagues." The clear inference is that they are less important than the rest of scripture. In fact, the label is a description of their size, not of their importance. When the scriptures were recorded on scrolls, the books we call the major prophets—heavy hitters like Isaiah, Jeremiah, or Ezekiel—each required an entire scroll. The prophetic works that were short enough to be combined onto one scroll became known as "The Twelve," or the minor prophets.

I think their brevity is to their advantage. Perhaps I think so because the major prophets intimidate me. They are like grand opera: so big, so long, and so loud that I steer clear of them, except during Advent and Lent when the lectionary and Handel's *Messiah* join forces to carry me into the poetry of Isaiah. The minor prophets are more accessible, each of them about the length of an average article in the *New York Times.*

Brendan Gill, theater critic for the *New Yorker,* once described a Broadway play as "a tiny little musical pretending to be a great big one." He criticized the "bizarre effect created by scaling pygmies up into giants." However, the minor prophets don't fall into that trap. They never pretend to be any bigger than they are. They seem to be content with their lot, standing in the shadows cast by the giants of biblical prophecy. They speak their word and fulfill their calling in the time and place to which God has called them. That is enough.

You may have opened this book the way I began my study: hesitant, curious, wondering if there was anything here to speak to our lives today. I discovered these books to be profoundly contemporary. Against the backdrop of an ancient culture, we catch a vision of human society that is yet to be realized. From the lips of forgotten prophets, we hear poetry that can lift us out of discouragement and into hope. In their struggle with oppression, injustice, political corruption, military power, and personal morality, we find renewed strength for the struggle that confronts men and women who seek God's justice in every age. Out of the depths of their absolute faith in Yahweh, the God of the Covenant, flows a deep river of living water to quench the thirst of our souls. As we encounter their calling to be God's spokespersons in their age, we experience the calling to become God's prophets in our own.

I offer this book as an introduction to the forgotten characters of biblical faith. I confess a blatant subjectivity: I introduce the prophets as I am experiencing them, reflecting the way their words inspire my soul, disturb my conscience, and enlarge my vision. What began as an attempt to hear them in their historical setting has become an occasion for hearing them in the present. My hope is that the witness of my own experience will encourage you to rediscover the prophets for yourself, to join me in listening to them in the present tense, to hear what they are saying to you today.

I am grateful to the people of St. Luke's United Methodist Church with whom I shared the earliest stages of this study. Our life together shaped these chapters for me, even as the interaction of the original prophets with their people shaped God's Word for them. The prophetic word came alive for me in the summer of 1990 with the invitation of Bishop Peter Storey to share in the ministry of Central Methodist Mission, Johannesburg, South Africa. The witness of that congregation is verifiable evidence that the Spirit who called the prophets of Israel continues to call prophetic witnesses today.

Orlando, Florida
Epiphany 1991

One

HURT INTO POETRY
The Calling of the Prophets

You were silly like us; your gift survived it all:
The parish of rich women, physical decay,
Yourself. Mad Ireland hurt you into poetry.
                                        —*W.H. Auden*

IN JANUARY OF 1939, W. H. AUDEN RECEIVED WORD of the death of his literary hero, Irish poet William Butler Yeats. Auden did what every poet does when he is moved by deep emotions of pain or joy: He wrote poetry. "In Memory of W.B. Yeats" describes the day of Yeats's death:

> What instruments we have agree
> The day of his death was a dark cold day.

When Auden said that Yeats was "hurt into poetry," he was describing the way the suffering, pain, and insanity of the world drove Yeats to write. To Auden, when Yeats verbalized the deepest emotions of his soul, it was poetry.

Yeats's experience was not unusual. It is almost axiomatic that great art emerges out of great suffering. John Steinbeck's masterpiece, *The Grapes of Wrath,* was born out of the novelist's personal outrage over the suffering of farm workers in California. Steinbeck walked the fields, visited the labor camps, and listened to the stories of the real men and women who became the fictional characters of his novel. During the winter of l939, Steinbeck labored for two weeks, sometimes day and night without rest, in Visalia, California, where thousands of starving people had been flooded out of their makeshift shelters. To his fellow traveler, Tom Collins, Steinbeck described the impact the experience had on his life. In his book, *Bringing in the Sheaves,* Collins notes Steinbeck as saying:

> ". . . heartbreaking. . . something hit me and hit me hard for it hurts inside clear to the back of my head. I got pains all over my head, hard pains. Have never had pains like this before . . . . "

In *Working Days,* Robert DeMott, the editor of the Steinbeck journals, credits the Visalia experience as the source of the novelist's greatest work.

> Clearly, Steinbeck's experience opened the floodgates of his attention, created *The Grapes of Wrath*'s compelling justification, provided its haunting spiritual urgency, and rooted it in the deepest wellsprings of democratic fellow-feelings. . . . the memory of Steinbeck's cataclysmic experience, his recollection of futility and impotency at Visalia, pervades the ending of the book and charges its ominous emotional climate . . . .

Many others have been hurt into poetry as well. Beethoven composed his greatest music in the silence of deafness. Milton shared his poetic vision out of his blindness.

Martin Luther King, Jr., wrote one of his clearest statements on social justice as a letter from the Birmingham city jail. *Cry, the Beloved Country* emerged out of Alan Paton's saturation with the pain of South Africa. Archbishop Desmond Tutu proclaims his vision of freedom in the crucible of injustice.

The poetry born out of pain is more than a cry of dereliction or a shout of anger. Auden's closing lines in tribute to Yeats describe the poet's task.

> Follow, poet, follow right
> To the bottom of the night,
> With your unconstraining voice
> Still persuade us to rejoice;
>
> With the farming of a verse
> Make a vineyard of the curse,
> Sing of human unsuccess
> In a rapture of distress;
>
> In the deserts of the heart
> Let the healing fountain start,
> In the prison of his days
> Teach the free man how to praise.

Auden knew the profound paradox of human suffering. The "healing fountain" starts in the "deserts of the heart." Real pain and real joy emerge from the same depths of the human soul. Those who know the tears of great pain also know the laughter of profound joy.

The Old Testament prophets followed the "human unsuccess" of their people into the desert of judgment; they knew the inevitable consequences of sin. Their witness to the faithfulness of God is set against the backdrop of the faithlessness of God's people. Their promise of restoration is born out of the ashes of destruction. Their call for justice rings through the tumult of oppression. Their scintillating vision of peace shines through ominous clouds of war. Beneath their penetrating words of judgment and through their journey into the wasteland of exile, throbs an irrefutable hope, a promise of healing and the first notes of praise.

At least 250 years separate the prophecy of Amos from the words of Malachi. Each prophet speaks to his own historical, political and religious circumstances, but they share several common characteristics.

First, the prophets each felt a personal sense of God's call. The Word of God came to them. Their ministry was not generated by their own power, but came from God. With the exception of Amos, for whom God's call came as a roaring lion, the call to the minor prophets was generally not as dramatic as it was for Isaiah, who "saw the Lord . . . sitting on his throne, high and exalted" (Isaiah 6:1). The minor prophets simply report that God spoke to them, revealing the divine purpose through their experiences.

Most of the prophets would probably have run from their calling if they could have avoided it. The satirical comedy of Jonah may, in fact, describe a reluctance common to all of them. But they were claimed by a Word that they did not create or control, a living Word that invaded their personalities and transformed their lives.

A second common mark of the prophets is an eschatological vision. Eschatology means seeing the present from the perspective of the future. It means confronting the realities of this day in the light of the ultimate purpose of God that one day will be fulfilled.

The Hebrew prophets differed from the neighboring cultures in their belief that history was linear, not cyclical. They believed that the God who made a covenant with Abraham was at work within history to move the world toward the complete realization of the divine purpose. In their vision, the drama ends with Yahweh as the triumphant King ruling over a world of *shalom*, the Hebrew word describing wholeness and peace. In the meantime, the covenant people are called to participate with God in accomplishing God's vision for the world. The realities of the present are to be constantly measured against God's vision for the future.

Third, the prophets' witness is marked by their actualization of this eschatological vision in their immediate circumstances. The prophets were not fortune-tellers, but they could see how actions in the present would have inevitable consequences in the future.

The biblical prophets dared to believe that behind and beneath the ruins of their life as a nation—the shattering defeats, the political upheaval, the disappointing failures, the dismal sins, and the painful corruption—the God of the Covenant was working through unsurmised strategies and rough-hewn trends to fulfill the promise of shalom. God was at work in their present circumstances to actualize the eschatological vision which would one day be fulfilled. God would not be finished with them until it was.

The prophets' task was to bring the life of the people into harmony with the purpose of God. To do it, they consistently called for personal and social repentance that would result in just and faithful living. As far as they could tell, everything mattered; every human decision either worked toward the fulfillment of God's purpose, bringing God's favor, or worked against it, incurring God's wrath. Their message was that faithful living results in blessing and unfaithful living results in judgment. The people were always free to choose.

The fourth common trait of the prophets was conflict. The application of God's vision to the present situation created then, as it creates today, inevitable conflict with existing powers of injustice and evil.

Biblical theologian Walter Wink studied Jesus' call to nonviolent change in the context of the struggle for justice in South Africa. In *Violence and Nonviolence in South Africa: Jesus' Third Way,* he wrote:

> Reduction of conflict by means of a phony "peace" is not a Christian goal. Justice is the goal, and that may require an acceleration of conflict as a necessary stage in forcing those in power to bring about genuine change.

Martin Luther King, Jr., following Gandhi's example, knew that "privileged groups rarely give up their privileges without strong resistance." Conflict is inevitable. The challenge is to face it without violence.

South African theologian John W. De Gruchy compared the witness of the church in South Africa to the witness of Dietrich Bonhoeffer in Nazi Germany, calling him a "troublesome witness for Jesus Christ."

> It was characteristic of Bonhoeffer that he so often went against the stream, even within his own circle. This was not simply because he had an independent and critical mind, or because he wanted to be different or difficult and go his own way. On the contrary, he so often found himself at odds with his contemporaries because of a developing and ever-deepening commitment to the truth of the gospel and its concrete implications in the midst of the world.

Like great artists in every age, the minor prophets were hurt into poetry. Through their pain they teach us to praise the God who is at work in human history to bring the fulfillment of the covenant vision for the whole world. As we follow their journey to "the bottom of the night," as we listen to them "sing of human unsuccess," as we go with them into "the deserts of the heart," may their "unconstraining voice still persuade us to rejoice" in the God who is not finished with us yet.

Two

LOVE THAT JUST WON'T QUIT
Hosea, Prophet of Relentless Love

I still believe that love is the most durable power in the world . . . . This principle stands at the center of the cosmos . . . . He who loves is a participant in the being of God. He who hates does not know God.

—Martin Luther King, Jr.

ADAM TRASK IS A VERY GOOD MAN. As the central character in John Steinbeck's *East of Eden,* he is so genuinely good that he is almost incapable of seeing the evil in others, particularly in Kate, who is as manipulative and selfish as Adam is generous and loving.

Beaten and left to die along the road, Kate stumbles onto the Trask porch. Adam nurses her back to health, falls in love with her, marries her, and takes her to California to begin a new life. After giving birth to twins, she shoots Adam, packs her bags and runs away. Years later Adam discovers that she is running a house of prostitution in the neighboring city.

Though he never wins her love, it is obvious that he still loves her and, as unbelievable as it seems, would have taken her back if she could have loved him in return.

Steinbeck's novel throbs with the same pathos as does the prophecy of Hosea. The theology of the prophet is autobiographical, his prophetic witness is revealed in his own pain-soaked marriage. In New Testament language, his story is incarnational: the word of the Lord becomes flesh through Hosea's love.

Hosea began his ministry during the reign of Jeroboam II (784-746 B.C.). Things were going well in the Northern Kingdom. The nation was at peace, the people were comfortable. But their prosperity rested on shallow foundations. The people were careless in their faith. During the reign of Jeroboam I, calf worship and the sensual rituals of the Baals were woven into their religious practices. The traditional Hebrew religious festivals became excuses for sexual abandon. The moral and ethical claims of the covenant were little more than a relic of the past.

Israel's peace and prosperity were soon disrupted by internal political intrigue as the external power of the Assyrians, under Tiglath-pileser, began to threaten their security. In 721 B.C., the Assyrians besieged the capital, Israel's armies were defeated, and the Northern Kingdom fell under Assyrian control.

Hosea saw these events as God's judgment upon the faithlessness and immorality of the nation. But throughout this time of defeat and despair, he continued to affirm the steadfast love of God.

Hosea shatters the popular stereotype of the prophets as mean-spirited purveyors of vengeance and anger. The central theme of his prophecy is captured in the Hebrew word *hesed,* a word usually translated "steadfast love." Hesed is a passionate, emotional, persistent loyalty. Although the lover sees clearly the beloved's unfaithfulness, *hesed* relentlessly works for the restoration of the relationship.

Hosea's wife, Gomer, was a prostitute. Scholars and preachers have exhausted themselves and their audiences debating whether or not Gomer was involved in "the oldest profession" before the marriage or became involved in it afterward. Old Testament scholar R. K. Harrison concludes:

> What is important to observe . . . is the fact that Hosea knew the waywardness of his wife from the very beginning of their marriage, just as God was aware of the infidelity of Israel from the time of the Wilderness period.

Gomer bore three children, their names reflecting the continuing tragedy of the life of the nation: Jezreel meaning "the destruction of Israel," Lo-Ruhamah meaning "no pity" or "no compassion," and Lo-Ammi meaning "not my people." After the children were born, Gomer returned to the streets.

Hosea pleads with his children to help him restrain her. He threatens punishment. He considers fencing her in with a wall and thorn bushes. But she keeps running to other men, selling herself to the highest bidder. Hosea is ready to throw in the towel, when he receives this command from the Lord:

> Go again and show your love for a woman who is committing adultery with a lover. You must love her just as I still love the people of Israel, even though they turn to other gods .
>
> —Hosea 3:1

Hosea continues to pursue her. In one of the most poignant scenes in scripture, he finds her on the auction block, being sold as a slave. Her beauty is gone. No longer the voluptuous young woman who could command the highest price from the men who lusted for her body, she has become a worn out, ragged, diseased, old whore, being offered to the highest bidder.

The auctioneer is ready to bring down the gavel when a voice calls from the back of the crowd, "Fifteen pieces of silver and seven bushels of barley." Everyone turns to see who would offer such an incredibly high price, far beyond anything the woman was worth. Imagine their amazement when they saw Hosea, buying back his unfaithful wife to take her home.

That is *hesed*. That is constant, steadfast love; love that just won't quit. And that, according to Hosea, is the love God has for the covenant people. God chose these people, claimed them as children, made a covenant to be faithful to them, and married them in the desert when he brought them out of bondage in Egypt. But they prostituted themselves by turning to other gods. Hosea heard the Lord say,

> They have left me. Like a woman who becomes a prostitute, they have given themselves to other gods.
>
> — Hosea 4:12.

The Lord describes their fickle love:

> What am I going to do with you? Your love for me disappears as quickly as morning mist; it is like dew, that vanishes early in the day. . . . What I want from you is plain and clear: I want your constant love [*hesed*], not your animal sacrifices. I would rather have my people know me than have them burn offerings to me.
>
> —Hosea 6:4-6

God's judgment is obvious here. The people will not escape the consequences of their behavior.

> My people are doomed because they do not acknowledge me.
>
> —Hosea 4:6
>
> When they sow the wind, they will reap a storm.
>
> —Hosea 8:7
>
> The people will get what they deserve.
>
> —Hosea 9:7

You planted evil and reaped its harvest. You have eaten the
fruit produced by your lies.

—Hosea 10:13

But behind, beneath, around, and through everything
else, Hosea feels the relentless, persistent love of God. In the
eleventh chapter, the analogy shifts from the love of a faithful
husband for an adulterous wife to the love of a patient father
for a rebellious child.

> The Lord says,
> "When Israel was a child, I loved him
> and called him out of Egypt as my son.
> But the more I called to him,
> the more he turned away from me.
>
> Yet I was the one who taught Israel to walk.
> I took my people up in my arms,
> but they did not acknowledge
> that I took care of them.
> I drew them to me with affection and love.
> I picked them up and held them to my cheek;
> I bent down to them and fed them."

—Hosea 11:1-4

This passionate God asks:

> How can I give you up, Israel?
> How can I abandon you?
>
> My heart will not let me do it!
> My love for you is too strong.
> I will not punish you in my anger;
> I will not destroy Israel again.
> For I am God and not man.
> I, the Holy One, am with you.
> I will not come to you in anger."

—Hosea 11:8-9

I wonder if Jesus was thinking of Hosea when he told the story of the loving father and the wandering son (Luke 15). Assuming that Jesus was a student of the Hebrew prophets, Hosea could be the literary origin of one of the best-known and best-loved stories Jesus ever told.

The closing words of Hosea's prophecy hold out the hope that one day this unswerving love will see the relationship restored.

> The Lord says,
> "I will bring my people back to me.
> I will love them with all my heart;
> ....
> I will be to the people of Israel
> like rain in a dry land.
> They will blossom like flowers;
> they will be firmly rooted
> like the trees of Lebanon.
> They will be alive with new growth,
> and beautiful like olive trees.
> Once again
> they will live under my protection.
> ....
> The people of Israel
> will have nothing more to do with idols;
> I will answer their prayers
> and take care of them.
> Like an evergreen tree
> I will shelter them;
> I am the source of all their blessings."
>
> —Hosea 14:4-8

Hosea hears the heartbroken cry of a God who loves deeply, faithfully, relentlessly, a God that cannot abandon the chosen people, even when they turn away. Hosea's prophecy lays to rests the common fiction that the God of the Old Testament is a God of judgment and the God of the New Testament is a God of love. With the single exception of the cross, there is no more powerful picture of the love of God than this passage from Hosea. The God revealed here is the same God of whom John would write:

See how much the Father has loved us! His love is so great that we are called God's children—and so, in fact, we are . . . . This is how we know what love is: Christ gave his life for us . . . . God showed his love for us by sending his only Son into the world, so that we might have life through him.
—1 John 3:1, 16; 4:9

The God who could not abandon the people of Israel has not given up on us. When we run from that love, when we sell ourselves to other lovers, when we prostitute ourselves for the sake of the pleasures of the world around us, that relentless love follows us. When we suffer the consequences of our own foolish choices, when we experience the results of our own human actions, that love surrounds us. When we get to the end of our rope and are being sold off cheap to the world around us, this God buys us back.

In spite of everything we do that results in evil for ourselves and others, this passionate, faithful God of *hesed* continues to see within us the possibility of restoration and renewal.

In *East of Eden,* Adam at last confronts Kate, seated at her desk in the bordello.

Adam stopped and slowly turned and his eyes were thoughtful. "I hadn't considered before," he said . . . . "Just now it came to me what you don't understand."

"What don't I understand, Mr. Mouse?"

"You know about the ugliness in people . . . . You use all the sad, weak parts of a man, and God knows he has them . . . . But you—yes, that's right—you don't know about the rest. . . . You don't believe I loved you. And the men who come to you here with their ugliness . . . you don't believe those men could have goodness and beauty in them. You see only one side, and you think—more than that, you're sure—that's all there is . . . . I seem to know that there's a part of you missing. Some men can't see the color green, but they may never know they can't . . . . But I wonder whether you ever feel that something invisible is all around you. It would be horrible if you knew it was there and couldn't see it or feel it. That would be horrible."

It would be horrible for us to be incapable of responding to the relentless love of God. But Hosea never gives up on the possibility that the people will return to God. He pleads with them:

> Return to the Lord your God, people of Israel. Your sin has made you stumble and fall. Return to the Lord, and let this prayer be your offering to him: "Forgive all our sins and accept our prayer, and we will praise you as we have promised . . . . We will never again say to our idols that they are our God. O Lord, you show mercy to those who have no one else to turn to."
>
> —Hosea 14:1-3

When I picture Hosea at the auction block bidding for his wife, my mind immediately recalls an old poem written by Myra Brooks Welch. It is travel weary but travels well.

> 'Twas battered and scarred, and the auctioneer
> Thought it scarcely worth his while
> To waste much time on the old violin,
> But he held it up with a smile.
> "What am I bidden, good folks," he cried,
> "Who will start bidding for me?
> A dollar, a dollar"—then, "Two!" "Only two?
> Two dollars, and who'll make it three?
> Three dollars once; three dollars, twice;
> Going for three—" but no,
> From the room, far back, a gray-haired man
> Came forward and picked up the bow;
> Then wiping the dust from the old violin,
> And tightening the loosened strings,

He played a melody pure and sweet
As sweet as a caroling angel sings.

The music ceased, and the auctioneer,
With a voice that was quiet and low,
Said, "What I am bidden for the old violin?"
And he held it up with the bow.
"A thousand dollars, and who'll make it two?
Two thousand! And who'll make it three?
Three thousand, once; three thousand, twice;
And going, and gone!" said he.
The people cheered, but some of them cried,
"We do not quite understand
What changed its worth?" Swift came the reply:
"The touch of the master's hand."

And many a man with life out of tune,
And battered and scattered with sin,
Is auctioned cheap to the thoughtless crowd,
Much like the old violin.
A "mess of pottage," a glass of wine;
A game—and he travels on.
He's "going" once, and "going" twice,
He's "going" and almost "gone."

But the Master comes, and the foolish crowd
Never can quite understand
The worth of a soul, and the change that's wrought
By the touch of the Master's hand.

That's *hesed*. That's love that just won't quit.

Three

THE ROAR OF THE LION
Amos, Prophet of Social Justice

*Mercy, detached from Justice, grows unmerciful
. . . . Mercy will flower only when it grows in
the crannies of the rock of Justice.*
—*C.S. Lewis*

ASLAN, THE LION, IS THE CHRIST-FIGURE in C.S. Lewis's marvelous children's stories *The Chronicles of Narnia.* When the children first hear of Aslan, Lucy asks, "Is—is he a man?"

> "Aslan a man!" said Mr. Beaver sternly. "Certainly not. I tell you he is the King of the wood and the son of the great Emperor-Beyond-the-Sea. Don't you know who is the King of Beasts? Aslan is a lion—<u>the</u> Lion, the great Lion."
>
> "Ooh!" said Susan, "I'd thought he was a man. Is he— quite safe? I shall feel rather nervous about meeting a lion."
>
> "That you will, dearie, and no mistake," said Mrs. Beaver, "if there's anyone who can appear before Aslan without their knees knocking, they're either braver than most or else just silly."

"Then he isn't safe?" said Lucy.

"Safe?" said Mr. Beaver . . . . "Who said anything about safe? 'Course he isn't safe. But he's good. He's the King, I tell you."

The first sound we hear in the prophecy of Amos is the roar of a lion: the lion of Judah, who is not safe, but who is very good.

> The Lord roars from Mount Zion;
> his voice thunders from Jerusalem.
> The pastures dry up, and
> the grass on Mount Carmel turns brown.
> ....
> Does a lion roar in the forest
> unless he has found a victim? . . .
> When a lion roars,
> who can keep from being afraid?
> When the Sovereign Lord speaks,
> who can keep from proclaiming his message?
> —Amos 1:2; 3:4, 8

Amos's imagery is brutally explicit when he describes the Lord's judgment on the people of Samaria:

> The Lord says, "As a shepherd recovers only two legs or an ear of a sheep that a lion has eaten, so only a few will survive of Samaria's people, who now recline on luxurious couches.
>
> How terrible it will be for you who long for the day of the Lord! . . . It will be a day of darkness and not of light. It will be like a man who runs from a lion and meets a bear!
> —Amos 3:12; 5:18-19

Amos begins with the lion's roar, the powerful image of the greatness and the absolute authority of the Almighty God.

> God is the one who made the mountains
> and created the winds.
> ....
> He walks the heights of the earth.
> This is his name: the Lord God Almighty!
>
> The Lord made the stars
> ....
> He calls for the waters of the sea
> and pours them out on the earth.
> His name is the Lord.
> He brings destruction on the mighty
> and their strongholds.
>
> The Sovereign Lord Almighty
> touches the earth, and it quakes.
> ....
> The whole world rises and falls
> like the Nile River.
> The Lord builds his home in the heavens,
> and over the earth
> he puts the dome of the sky.
> He calls for the waters of the sea
> and pours them out on the earth.
> His name is the Lord!
>
> —Amos 4:13; 5:8-9; 9:5-6

Yahweh is not a soft, cuddly deity who keeps us comfortable and secure in our cozy, little world. The Lord is not a celestial bellhop, waiting to service our needs or do our bidding. This is the great God of creation, the eternal God of history, the awesome God of all power who is infinitely good and unerringly just. Amos's prophetic call is rooted in his profound awareness of the immutable goodness of God.

If this sounds like heady theology that floats about fifteen feet off the floor, let me remind you of the practical difference this awareness can make in human behavior. As special prosecutor for the Watergate scandal, Leon Jaworski listened to the infamous tapes on which the voices of the President and his aides revealed the corruption of the Nixon White House. In *The Right and the Power* Mr. Jaworski reflected on the theological significance of those tapes.

> THE TAPES! The teaching of right and wrong were forgotten in the White House. Little evils were permitted to grow into great evils, small sins escalated into big sins. In the hours and hours of tape-recorded conversations to which I listened, not once was there a reference to the Glory of God, not once a reference to seeking spiritual guidance through prayer. Our Lord was mentioned, yes, but on each pitiable occasion His name was taken in vain. If only there had been an occasional prayer for help, an occasional show of compassion! Why was there not just a simple statement such as: "May we hold our honor sacred . . . " How different might have been the course of government if there had been an acknowledgment of God as the source of right instead of a denial of Him in a seemingly unending series of ruthless actions.

Twenty-seven hundred years before Watergate, Amos came to the people of Israel with the same conviction. Human life is corrupted and the moral order unhinged when we refuse to acknowledge the greatness and goodness of God. The prophet's call for the reordering of the social, political, moral, and religious life of his people is rooted in the moral character of the Almighty. Amos will not allow us to settle for a socially acceptable, convenient little deity who is wheeled on and off the stage at our whim or desire. He calls us back to the all-powerful God who formed the world and ultimately rules human history.

God's judgment of sin is grounded in the fact that Yahweh has specifically acted on behalf of the covenant people and therefore has every right to hold them accountable for their actions. The Lord declares:

And yet, my people, it was for your sake that I . . . brought you out of Egypt, led you through the desert for forty years, and gave you the land of the Amorites to be your own.

Of all the nations on earth, you are the only one I have known and cared for. That is what makes your sins so terrible and that is why I must punish you for them.

—Amos 2:9-10; 3:2

Behind God's judgment is God's monumental act of grace. Before God's call to repentance is God's gift of liberation. Prior to God's punishment is God's love. John Wesley, the founder of Methodism, spoke of "prevenient grace," describing God's grace that is always prior to our response. The first act in the drama is God's act of deliverance. God has earned the right to call his people to faithful living because God has already been faithful to them.

God's faithfulness is the basis for the indictment against Israel:

The Lord says, "The people of Israel have sinned again and again, and for this I will certainly punish them. They sell into slavery honest men who cannot pay their debts, poor men who cannot repay even the price of a pair of sandals. They trample down the weak and helpless and push the poor out of the way. A man and his father have intercourse with the same slave girl, and so profane my holy name."

—Amos 2:6-7

For the prophet, sin against another person is sin against God. God's name is profaned when people abuse, oppress, or inflict suffering on others. Faithful living is evidenced not only in religious practice, but in human relationships, social responsibilities, and the economic and political structures of society.

Amos understood that most of us are visual learners. His prophecy fills the screen of imagination with effective visual images of the truth he proclaims. One day he noticed a builder testing the straightness of a wall with his plumb line. The Spirit went to work in his imagination.

> "Amos, what do you see?" the Lord asks.
>   "A plumb line," the prophet responds.
>   "I am using it to show that my people are like a wall that is out of line."
>
> —Amos 7:8

The Hebrew root for the word justice means "straightness" in a physical sense. Biblical justice is the moral and ethical standard by which God measures human conduct. It is the plumb line of God's goodness dropped into the middle of every human situation, revealing where our lives are crooked, unbalanced, out of line.

In her satirical revue *Like It Is!,* Helen Kromer brings the prophet on stage as he drops his plumb line into the common experiences of contemporary life. The chorus sings:

> The plumb line, the plumb line
> It just came plummeting down.
> Marking the line as plumb lines do
> As absolutely vertically true
> And setting askew as plumb lines do
> A vast amount of what everyone thought
> were the vertically absolute parts
> of the rest of town.

After a vigorous debate with the prophet about the real effects of that plumb line in their experiences, the people conclude:

> He is setting a plumb line
> in the center of the city.
> For he means to build us straight
> and He means to build us just.
> He has chosen His people
> and He means to make us upright;

> he is dropping in a plummet
> for the sounding out of us.

One morning Amos was hiking through the hills when he came upon a waterfall. As he watched the water tumble out of the earth, he heard the Spirit say, "Let justice roll down like waters, and righteousness like an everflowing stream" (Amos 5:24 *NRSV*).

Amos is absolutely convinced that God's justice will be accomplished. You cannot stop it any more than you can stop the water from flowing over Niagara Falls. The prophet has no doubt about that. The only question is how faithfully the people will participate in its coming.

One of Thomas Jefferson's most painful defeats came in 1784 when his bill banning slavery in the new territories was defeated in Congress by one vote. He questioned:

> Can the liberties of a nation be thought secure when we have removed their only firm basis, a conviction in the minds of the people that these liberties are the gift of God? That they are not to be violated but with His wrath?
>
> Indeed I tremble for my country when I reflect that God is just; that his justice cannot sleep forever.

The writer of the Declaration of Independence shared Amos's conviction that God's justice would one day be fulfilled.

> We must await with patience the workings of an overruling Providence, and hope that is preparing the deliverance of these, our suffering brethren. When the measure of their tears shall be full, when their groans shall have involved heaven itself in darkness, doubtless a God of justice will awaken to their distress, and by diffusing light and liberality among their oppressors, or, at length, by his exterminating thunder manifest his attention to the things of this world, and that they are not left to the guidance of a blind fatality.

In the struggle for justice and equality, men and women of faith continue to envision a day when "justice rolls down like waters."

My personal involvement with the Methodists of South Africa began at the World Methodist Conference in Nairobi, Kenya, in 1986. One of the most memorable moments for me was the witness of Bishop Peter Storey. He concluded his message with a ringing word of confidence in the ultimate justice of God, addressed directly to then-President of South Africa, P.W. Botha.

> Let me now witness from this platform of World Methodism to those in places of power in Pretoria, to that Government which, deaf to Christian conscience and blind to human consequence, has taken the dark impulses which you and I know lie in every heart and written them into the law of the land—which has brought the Beloved Country to disaster. Let me say to Mr. Botha, "Apartheid is doomed!" . . . Apartheid is the god that has failed.
>
> Let me say to Mr. Botha . . . "In the name of the one true God, the God of Abraham, Isaac and Jacob, the God and Father of our Lord Jesus Christ—stop! Stop this evil thing! Open the prison doors! Call the exiles home! Burn the population register with its pornographic classifications of God's children by the colour of their skin! Do it now! For as sure as God lives and as Jesus is Lord, you will have to do it in the end!"

The words resonated with the Spirit who spoke through the eighth century Hebrew prophets, but the bishop himself did not expect the prophecy to be fulfilled as quickly as it was. Only four years later, a new president of South Africa released Nelson Mandela, welcomed exiles home, and began negotiations for the end of apartheid. The vision is not yet fulfilled, but the work of transformation has begun.

The prophecy that begins with the roar of a lion concludes on a note of exuberant hope. The same Lord who held the plumb line of judgment promises:

I will restore the Kingdom of David,
which is like a house fallen into ruins.
I will repair its walls and restore it.
I will rebuild it
and make it as it was long ago.

They will rebuild their ruined cities
and live there;
they will plant vineyards and drink the wine;
they will plant gardens
and eat what they grow.
I will plant my people
on the land I gave them,
and they will not be pulled up again."

—Amos 9:11, 14-15

Amos closes the way he began, with the roar of the lion: "The Lord your God has spoken!"

Four

WHEN YOU SEE
TOMORROW COME
Micah, Visionary Prophet
of Peace

*It may be that the day of judgment will dawn
tomorrow; in that case, we shall gladly stop
working for a better future. But not before.*
—*Dietrich Bonhoeffer*

THE BROADWAY MUSICAL VERSION of the Victor Hugo
novel *Les Miserables* was a powerful religious experience for
me. In the closing scene, Jean Valjean, the story's hero, is
dying. As he breathes his last breath, the ghosts of the men and
women he has loved and with whom he has struggled for
justice and freedom gather around him. They drift onto the
stage singing softly:

> Do you hear the people sing,
> Lost in the valley of the night?
> It is the music of a people
> Who are climbing to the light.

> For the wretched of the earth
> There is a flame that never dies.
> Even the darkest night will end
> And the sun will rise.

The orchestra joins the chorus and the rhythm builds as the ghostly singers paraphrase the words of Micah:

> They will live again in freedom
> In the garden of the Lord.
> They will walk behind the plowshares,
> They will put away the sword.
> The chains will be broken
> And all men will have their reward.

With the final crescendo, they offer this challenge:

> Will you join in our crusade?
> Who will be strong and stand with me?
> Somewhere beyond the barricade
> Is there a world you long to see?
> Do you hear the people sing?
> Say, do you hear the distant drum?
> It is the future that they bring
> When tomorrow comes.

The music captures the passion for liberation that swept across France in the eighteenth century and the same spirit of liberation that we witnessed in Eastern Europe, the Soviet Union, South Africa and China in 1989. It is the same passion that enflamed Micah's prophecy in eighth century B.C. Micah was among the first prophets to proclaim the vision of how this world will look when God's tomorrow comes.

The Hebrew root word for prophet is the same as the verb that translates "to see." The prophets could see God's purpose being worked out in the social, economic, and political realities of their nation. They recognized the inevitable consequences of the corruption of their society.

They could envision their present experience from the perspective of God's vision for the future.

Micah describes his prophetic role:

> But as for me, I am filled with power
> Through the Spirit of the Lord!
> I can see what is just and right,
> And I have the strength to declare it.
> —Micah 3:8, *J.B. Phillips*

Like Hosea, Micah saw the people drifting from their love for God; he decried their prostitution with the pagan gods, and he called for purity in religious practice. Like Amos, he saw rampant injustice, corruption in the courts, oppression of the poor, and the arrogant coldheartedness of the powerful toward the powerless, and he renewed the call for "justice to roll down like waters and righteousness like an everflowing stream."

With the rest of the pre-exilic prophets, Micah saw the political turmoil within his own nation and the impending invasion of Assyria. But in the seething caldron of his time, Micah could also see God's tomorrow coming.

> In days to come
> the mountain where the Temple stands
> will be the highest of all,
> towering above all the hills.
> Many nations will come streaming to it,
> and their people will say,
> "Let us go up the hill of the Lord,
> to the Temple of Israel's God.
> For he will teach us what he wants us to do;
> we will walk in the paths he has chosen."
> ....
> He will settle disputes among the nations,
> among the great powers near and far.
> They will hammer their swords into plows
> and their spears into pruning knives.

Nations will never again go to war,
never prepare for battle again.
Everyone will live in peace among his own
vineyards and fig trees,
and no one will make him afraid.
The Lord Almighty has promised this.

—Micah 4:1-4

That is the vision. That is what God's tomorrow will look like. For Micah, all forms of violence are a compromise with evil. In God's vision there is no "holy" war; all forms of militarism, though sometimes inevitable or unavoidable because of human failure and sin, are a temporary bargain with Satan that falls short of God's intention for the created order.

God envisions a world where swords are turned into plows and spears are used for pruning knives; where the implements of war become garden tools to produce food; where dollars now spent on bombs are spent on babies; where the money set aside for space weapons provides therapy for drug abusers, health care for the elderly, and medical care for AIDS patients; where the only thing we store in silos is grain to feed the world's hungry; where the best scientific minds will work together to find a cure for cancer rather than searching for a more terrifying means of destruction; where resources no longer directed toward death will be energized for life; where no one will go to bed afraid. The Lord Almighty promises it!

But even as the music of those who would struggle for justice and freedom rings in our ears, we tune in the evening news and watch the nations of the world unload their soldiers and weapons in some far-off corner of the world. We walk down the violence-filled streets of our cities, build our walls and install security systems in our homes, and know how far this world is from the fulfillment of God's vision of peace. Sometimes God's shalom seems like a beautiful dream that evaporates in the brutal clarity of the noonday sun. Micah's

world looked that way, too. His description reads like the
front page of the *New York Times*.

> When morning comes, as soon as they have the chance,
> they do the evil they planned. When they want fields, they
> seize them; when they want houses, they take them. No
> man's family or property is safe.
>
> Listen, you rulers of Israel! You are supposed to be
> concerned about justice, yet you hate what is good and love
> what is evil.
>
> Your rich men exploit the poor, and all of you are liars.
>
> There is not an honest person left in the land, no one
> loyal to God . . . . They are all experts at doing evil.
> Officials and judges ask for bribes. The influential man tells
> them what he wants, and so they scheme together. Even the
> best and most honest of them are as worthless as weeds.
>
> —Micah 2:1-2; 3:1-2; 6:12; 7:2-4

Micah spoke to a violence-prone world perched on the
brink of war, dominated by military power, ruled by force,
infected with corruption and injustice. A world not so very
different from our own.

We experienced the violence in our world on our first
morning on the streets of Johannesburg. We were seven very
American tourists, walking through streets where tourists
seldom go, experiencing the immediate parish of Central
Methodist Mission. Around the corner from the bus terminal,
the sidewalk became more crowded. In the human avalanche,
Fran, the smallest woman in our group, became separated
from the rest of us. Instantly, two men grabbed her from
behind. One strong arm wrapped around her shoulders. A
huge hand yanked the gold chain from around her neck while
another pulled on the purse that was hanging from her
shoulder. In less time than it takes to describe the incident, the
muggers were disappearing again into the crowd.

As we waited in the police station to bandage her
wounds and file the reports, I realized that all of us had
changed. We were no longer observers of the problems of the

city, we had become participants. Fear of violence was no longer a topic for objective study, but a subjective reality. We had become the helpless victims of the world's violence.

With Micah's first hearers we ask: What can I do? The world's violence is so complicated and so pervasive, and I'm just one little insignificant person. What does the Lord expect me to do? The prophet's answer is disarmingly simple and incisively profound:

> He has told you, O mortal, what is good;
> and what does the Lord require of you
> but to do justice, and to love kindness,
> and to walk humbly with your God?
> —Micah 6:8, *NRSV*

Micah calls us to live today on the basis of what we believe about tomorrow, to shape our lives in the present in ways that are consistent with God's vision for the future; to stop living on the basis of what has always been, and to start living on the basis of God's new way of justice, mercy and peace.

Micah was a small town boy from an out of the way village named Moresheth, tucked away in the southern lowlands of Judah. Micah knew about small places, and he dared to believe that God could use small things in a big way. Seven hundred years before the birth of Jesus he could believe that even a nowhere place like Bethlehem could produce a ruler for the people of Israel who would bring peace (Micah 5:2-5). Even small things, little people, and folks from out of the way places like Moresheth and Bethlehem can share in the coming of God's tomorrow of justice and peace.

In *The Merchant of Venice,* William Shakespeare wrote: "How far that little candle throws his beam!/So shines a good deed in a naughty world."

And Jesus, the country boy from a little town called Bethlehem, told us that all it takes is faith like the mustard seed, the smallest seed of all, to be a part of the kingdom of

God. Micah's call is for ordinary people to do what they can, where they can, to fulfill the vision of God. The promise is that God can use small things in a powerful way to move human life toward God's shalom.

The Methodist Order of Peacemakers is a small company of South African Christians who are taking Jesus' words about peacemaking and nonviolence very seriously. I can remember their faces and their stories.

Richard was the first person imprisoned for refusing military service. His body still bears the evidence of his incarceration.

Eric is a law school graduate and conscientious objector who spent three years as a filing clerk in alternative service who now uses his training to study the complicity of the security forces in the nation's violence.

Wayne is a university student from Namibia who was held in detention during the state of emergency. At times, his eyes seemed to reveal a frightened, darting look.

Andre is a young pastor who is wrestling with how he will respond if called to serve in the military in light of his commitment to peace and his responsibility for a wife and children.

Alan is a soul friend and brother in Christ, who spent a year in Australia wrestling with his response to the law requiring every 18-year-old white male to register for a year in military service or face six years in prison. In 1989 he returned home as a Christian pacifist, committed to Jesus' way of nonviolence. He said simply, "Jesus chose nonviolence and I must do the same . . . . The ends I desire must be seen in the means I use." He notified the defense forces that if drafted, he would refuse to serve.

In the fall of 1990, while terrifying violence was sweeping across Johannesburg, Alan's draft notice came.

> On the 1st of October I received my Call Up papers. They want me in Upington in the infantry. I've waited two years for that letter—but when I got it I was shocked—like I

have to rethink over everything I believe in. On the other hand I was relieved—it's been a long time in coming. As I have thought over it these past days—I am more and more convinced that God's timing is good. I am now a "man of the cloth" so to speak [He is a candidate for ordination in The Methodist Church of Southern Africa] which makes a big difference in the public perception of one as well as giving me a greater support base. It's as if it is not only me but the whole Methodist Church making a stand. I also feel in these transforming days—days filled with our worst ever violence—that a stand against conscription—a statement of faith in Jesus instead of force—is vital. So I praise God for the possible opportunity to voice my faith in Jesus . . . . I am busy writing a full statement of conscience and organizing a support group just in case I find myself in court.

Little did Alan realize when he received notification of his call up that in less than twenty-four hours his commitment to Christ-like, redemptive nonviolence would be tested on the streets of Johannesburg.

That night (1 October) I was attacked [near] one of the Shabeens [illegal drinking establishments on the street corners of the city]. A man came from behind me, grabbed my bag and lunged at my head with a knife. They often go for the head so that blood prevents you from identifying them. Somehow, God only knows, only the handle of the knife made contact with my head, leaving a small cut. I moved about 10m [meters] away from him and asked him if he had a problem. Just then two plain clothes police people jumped on him from behind. They began kicking him; one jumped on his head. I kept on shouting, "Don't hurt him," and had to hold one of the police back before they stopped. Justifying violence makes redemption impossible to take place! I mean, how could I speak about forgiveness to that man while his head was split open?

Will the efforts of the Methodist Peacemakers bring the South African Defense Force to a grinding halt? Of course not. Will their witness for peace put an end to the violence that rages around them? I doubt it. But God is using their witness in an unmistakable way. They are living today in ways that are consistent with God's vision of tomorrow.

The prophetic invitation still comes to us, the music still rings in our ears:

> Will you join in our crusade?
> Who will be strong and stand with me?
> Somewhere beyond the barricade
> Is there a world you long to see?
> So you hear the people sing?
> Say, do you hear the distant drum?
> It is the future that they bring
> When tomorrow comes.

Five

HOW BIG IS YOUR WORLD?
Jonah, Reluctant Prophet of
Boundless Concern

The world stands out on either side
No wider than the heart is wide;
Above the world is stretched the sky,
No higher than the soul is high.
　　　　　—Edna St. Vincent Millay

WHAT CAN YOU DO WITH A GUY LIKE JONAH? He is the Archie Bunker of the Old Testament, the exaggerated stereotype of prejudice and bigotry, the kind of character who makes you lean back, take a deep breath, and ask, "Can you believe this guy?"

Jonah's story can be read as ancient Hebrew hyperbole, in the same vein as Jesus' comical images of a camel going through the eye of the needle, or the guy who was so busy pointing out the speck of sawdust in his brother's eye that he couldn't see the two-by-four in his own. The operating assumption is that while we are laughing at the absurdity, we will see just how foolish we are.

Jonah was a real prophet who lived in the later part of the eighth century B.C. (2 Kings 14:25). The story as we have it probably emerged after the Exile. The Hebrew storytellers picked up the historical character of Jonah, stretched the story to absurd proportions, and hoped that while people were laughing, they would begin to discover that the story was directed at them. It is a Hebrew story, about a Hebrew prophet, addressed to Hebrew people. It is a well-honed folk drama in three acts.

Act I: God calls Jonah, just as God called the other prophets, but his call is unique in two ways. First of all, Jonah was called to go to Nineveh, which is a Gentile, not a Hebrew city. Secondly, Jonah said, "No." He turns in the opposite direction and heads for the seaport of Joppa, buys a ticket and sails for Spain.

While Jonah is making the crossing, a storm comes up on the sea. The sailors pray to all the gods they can think of, and when they have tried everything they know, they wake up their passenger and tell him to pray to his god to see if it will do any good. When they ask his nationality, Jonah puffs up his ancestral pride and announces, "I am a Hebrew. I worship the Lord, the God of heaven who made the land and sea" (Jonah 1:9). Then Jonah confesses that he is running away from God and that the storm is probably because of him. He tells the sailors to throw him overboard. These pagan sailors show more compassion for Jonah than he showed for the people of Nineveh. They first refuse to toss him over the side, but when the ship is about to sink, they finally give in, and into the sea goes Jonah.

The next scene is the only thing most folks remember about Jonah. He is swallowed by a "huge fish." As I researched this part of the story, I was amazed at the lengths to which some people go to try to prove the literal truth of this scene. They have studied the sea life of the period, measured fish fossils, and collected stories of other sailors who were swallowed and then regurgitated into the ocean. It is all fascinating stuff, but reading through it is like listening to a specialist in contagious diseases analyze a kiss. If you think about it too much, you take all the fun out of it and miss the point.

The truth in the story is larger than the digestive tract of the fish. It is best to take the story on its own terms, let it speak to you, and not get hung up on the literal difficulties of floating around in the stomach of a whale.

Evidently, at least, Jonah soon got the point. From the belly of the whale he prays to God to deliver him, which at the very least suggests that Jonah caught on that life is the pits when we try to run from God. At the end of Act I, the whale has had all it can stand of Jonah and spews him up on the shore.

Act II: God calls Jonah again and tells him to get going on his way to Nineveh. Frankly, if I had been God I think I would have tried to find another boy, but this is, after all, the God who just won't quit. With the smell of fish guts still lingering in his nostrils, Jonah goes to Nineveh, complaining all the way. He proclaims God's word: Clean up your act or God is going to destroy the city in forty days. To Jonah's surprise, these unbelieving, sinful, Gentile people of Nineveh believe him! They repent, they fast, they put on sackcloth, and they turn things around, which is more than we have seen the chosen people do. God sees their response, changes his mind, and decides not to punish them. Everyone is happy. Everyone except Jonah.

Act III: As the curtain goes up, the prophet is complaining again. In fact, the Bible says that Jonah was angry with God. "Lord," he says, "this is just what I knew would happen! This is why I tried to run away to Spain! I knew that you were loving and merciful, even to outsiders, Gentiles and sinners like the people of Nineveh. You are always kind and patient, always ready to change your mind and not punish folks if they turn to you. And that's just what you did, darn it! I'd rather be dead than see Nineveh saved from destruction!"

He goes out of the city, and sits down to sulk. But God isn't finished with Jonah. He makes a vine grow up to shade him. Jonah likes it. The next morning, however, a worm attacks the vine, it dies, and the sun starts to beat down on Jonah. Again, the prophet is angry and wishes he were dead. The story closes with God saying:

> What right do you have to be angry? . . . This plant grew up in one night and disappeared the next; you didn't do anything for it and you didn't make it grow—yet you feel sorry for it! How much more, then should I have pity on Nineveh, that great city. After all, it has more than 120,000 innocent children in it, as well as many animals!
>
> —Jonah 4:9-10

With that, the curtain falls.

What are you going to do with a story like that? What can you do with a character like Jonah?

Elie Wiesel, the Jewish poet of the Holocaust, reminds us that this story is included in the readings for the Jewish celebration of Yom Kippur, the days of repentance. He suggests it is there, first, for comic relief, and, second, because it is a story about repentance.

Repentance—turning in a new direction—is always possible. Biblical faith believes that life is not an inevitable march toward destruction. It is always possible for us to change, to leave our past and move toward a new future. The story of Jonah reveals the way repentance brought new life for the city of Nineveh, and how the lack of repentance—Jonah's stubborn refusal to see the world through the eyes of God's inclusive love—leaves a person hard, cold, and desolate. Wiesel writes:

> Repentance means that fate is not inexorable, decisions are never irrevocable. Man is not a toy whose function is prearranged; his link to infinity assures him access to endless possibilities . . . . the cycle of crime and punishment can be halted before it is completed. Evil can be aborted, diverted,

vanquished. Better yet, it can be transformed; it can undergo endless mutations—by choosing repentance.

But if this is a story about repentance, what is the specific change, the new direction to which the story calls us?

The tale of Jonah is not about what happens when a particular prophet was swallowed by a whale; it is about what happens to any man or woman who is swallowed by narrow, nationalistic, ethnic, or racial pride. It is a story about jingoism—an unhealthy love of nation or race that turns in on itself and becomes sick and destructive.

Jonah's story is the comic portrayal of religious and racial jingoism, in stark contrast to the universal, inclusive love of God. The inescapable point of the story for its Hebrew storytellers was that although God had chosen the people of Israel to be the bearers of the covenant, God's love was for the whole creation. God's relationship with Israel was the model of what God intended for the whole world.

Yahweh is the God of unbounded compassion, unrestrained by boundaries of nations, unhindered by definitions of race or clan, unhampered by ethnic and social traditions, utterly disrespectful of the ways we separate people by political convictions or economic assumptions. God's people can either get on board with that love, or they can sit around under their withering vines and dry up in the sun.

The New Testament parallel to this story is recorded in the tenth chapter of Acts. Cornelius was a captain in the Roman guard. Like the people of Nineveh, he was a Gentile, an outsider. But he was also a good man, a man who worshipped God and who helped the poor Jewish people. One day he received a vision in which an angel told him that God had heard his prayers and was ready to answer him. He was to send messengers to find Peter in Joppa.

Back in Joppa, the same port from which Jonah had set sail, Peter is on the roof taking a nap. In a dream, he sees a huge sheet being lowered from heaven, weighted down with all kinds of animals, reptiles and wild birds. A voice commands, "Kill and eat."

Like Jonah saying no to God, Peter shouts back, "Certainly not, Lord! I have never eaten anything ritually unclean." The voice replies, "Do not consider anything unclean that God has declared clean."

Just about that time, Peter is awakened by a knock at the door. It is the servants of the Roman army captain. In contrast to Jonah, Peter comes to his senses and says, "You yourselves know very well that a Jew is not allowed by his religion to visit or associate with Gentiles. But God has shown me that I must not consider any person ritually unclean or defiled" (Acts 10:28).

Peter learns the lesson Jonah refused to learn: "I now realize that it is true that God treats everyone on the same basis" (Acts 10:34). He proclaims the good news of Jesus and concludes with this bold affirmation: "Everyone who believes in him will have his sins forgiven through the power of his name" (Acts 10:43).

Both Jonah and Peter begin with jingoism, but whereas Jonah ends up sulking under his dead vine, Peter ends up rejoicing in the power of universal love. Both stories force us to ask: How big is our world? How wide is our love? How large is our compassion?

One of Peter Storey's favorite stories is of the day he took communion to Ike Moloabi, a black pastor who was imprisoned during the state of emergency. They met in a corner of the prison with a huge Afrikaner guard who monitored their conversation. When it came time to share the Eucharist, Peter told the guard that we Methodists always have an open table and he was welcome to join them. Because the Afrikaners are terribly religious people, the guard could not refuse.

Peter passed the cup to Ike and he drank. The cup was then passed to the prison guard, who suddenly realized that if he wanted to receive the grace of God, he would have to place his lips on a cup from which a black man had just drunk.

That would be unheard of in South Africa. But after a moment of hesitation, he took the cup and drank.

Then, with a twinkle in his eye, Peter said that we Methodists always hold hands to say the closing prayer, and, as he did so, he silently asked the Lord to help him keep a straight face as he watched the prisoner and the prison guard hold hands. After his release, Ike told Peter that the guard had been different in his treatment of him from that point on.

Mahin Root is a 14-year-old student in Greensboro, North Carolina, who went to register in the public school not too long ago and ended up causing quite a stir. The problem first went to the local school board, then the state office, and now it is floating around in Washington somewhere. It was all because she politely refused to fill in one line on the registration form, the line that asked for her race. She refused to fill in the line for two reasons. One was that she has a black mother and a white father, and she wasn't sure what to put down. The second reason was that she and her family have a profound religious conviction that, as she says, "There is only one race—the human race."

The same Spirit who called Jonah to go to Nineveh is still at work in human history to bring repentance and healing to broken relationships in the human family. Because ultimately, that is how God sees the human race—as one race. That is the lesson God tried to teach Jonah, that is the lesson Peter learned in Joppa, and it is God's lesson for us.

Six

MINE EYES
HAVE SEEN THE GLORY
Nahum, Prophet of Judgment

The church is the first to feel the disturbing
tremors of God's work in history in order that
it might be renewed and become a sign of hope
for the world. If the church can . . . perceive the
grace of God within his acts of wrath, then it
may well begin to be an instrument of his
justice and peace, and a sign of hope.
                                    —*John W. DeGruchy*

IF I HAD BEEN THERE in the second and third centuries when the early church was deciding which books to include and which to leave out of the canon of holy scripture, I probably would have left Nahum out. My first impression was that this little book contains just about everything that turns people away from the Old Testament.

The prophecy opens with an eloquent poem about the anger and power of God (Nah. 1:2-10), which is then applied with a vengeance to the city of Nineveh; its vision of destruction standing in brazen contrast to Micah's vision of peace; its vengeance upon the Assyrians sounding like a noisy contradiction of the universal compassion of Jonah.

The prophet's exact identity is lost to us; we know nothing of his personal life. However, the historical situation he confronts is clear. For more than a century, Assyrian military might had held the ancient Middle East in its brutal power. Judah came under direct Assyrian control in 734 B.C. In 722 B.C., the ten Hebrew tribes of the Northern Kingdom were erased from the pages of history. A crushed revolt in the days of Hezekiah (715-687 B.C.) resulted in economic bankruptcy with the payment of heavy tribute to the Assyrian ruler, Sennacherib. Under Manasseh (687-642 B.C.) there was widespread injustice in the courts, Assyrian gods and goddesses were brought into the Temple, the prophets were persecuted, child sacrifice was instituted, and the people adopted Assyrian religious customs and dress. Long after the people forgot the man named Nahum, they continued to pass on the prophecy which sees Assyria as the embodiment of ruthless, arrogant, militaristic power that contradicts the goodness of God.

The Assyrian might began to crumble with the sacking of Thebes in 663 B.C., to which Nahum specifically refers (Nah. 3:8), culminating in the fall of the Assyrian capital of Nineveh in 612 B.C., the event upon which Nahum's vision focuses. The book ends with the proclamation that all who hear the story of Nineveh's fall will clap their hands for joy, celebrating the ironic end of Assyria's "endless cruelty" (Nah. 3:19).

The key to Nahum's prophecy is the opening hymn of praise (Nah. 1:2-10) that focuses our attention squarely on the power of God. In the fall of Nineveh, Nahum sees a graphic illustration of the way the God works in the history of nations to defeat arrogance, evil, injustice, brutality, and oppression.

Now most of us would never use adjectives like jealous and avenging to describe God. But the prophet does not hesitate to use forceful language to describe God's confrontation with the evil powers of this world.

> A jealous and avenging God is the Lord,
> the Lord is avenging and wrathful;
> the Lord takes vengeance on his adversaries
> and rages against his enemies.
> Who can stand before his indignation?
> Who can endure the heat of his anger?
> His wrath is poured out like fire,
> and by him the rocks are broken in pieces.
> —Nahum 1:2, 6, *NRSV*

Nahum is, first and last, a witness to the absolute power and goodness of God, a God whose power is directed toward shalom and against any person, nation, or force that contradicts that goodness or thwarts that purpose. The prophet is far more comfortable with a jealous and avenging God whose wrath is turned against evil than with a world where ruthless power has its way with impunity.

During the difficult days of the early 1940's, while Hitler was gobbling up most of central Europe, Dr. Harry Emerson Fosdick preached a memorable sermon at Riverside Church in New York City entitled "Why Is God Silent While Evil Rages?" He reminded the radio congregation across the nation of the silent power that "works inevitable retribution upon evil."

> Like it or not, in this universe there is what the ancient Greeks called Nemesis—the doom that, however long delayed, falls upon arrogance and cruelty and braggart pride . . . . God does not sit in heaven and do nothing. We frail human beings are not alone the originators, improvisers, and backers of goodness in this world.

The good news from Nahum is that the full power of the almighty God will ultimately support goodness and defeat evil. Ruthless tyranny, arrogant power, and brutal repression hold the seeds of their own destruction. Behind the disturbing contrast between Nahum, who was gloating over the bloody destruction of Nineveh, and Jonah, who was complaining about God's mercy toward the same city, is the historically-proven truth of Jesus' words: "All who take the sword will perish by the sword" (Matt. 26:52, *NRSV*). The judgment of God against ruthless violence is written into the fabric of human history.

It is one thing for Nahum to see this judgment directed toward the Assyrians. It is only the most profound biblical faith that dares to see it directed toward one's own nation. After a destructive bombing raid against Berlin, Dietrich Bonhoeffer wrote from his prison cell to Eberhard Bethge:

> Never have we been so plainly conscious of the wrath of God, and that it is a sign of his grace: O that today you would hearken to his voice! Harden not your hearts!

Seen from the perspective of the inevitable fall of arrogant power, even Nahum's horrifying vision of the destruction of Nineveh can be seen as God's judgment against the brutality and violence that Assyrian power represented. It can serve as an unexpected reminder that violence ultimately produces more violence. We cannot ultimately obtain goodness through evil means; we cannot accomplish shalom through war.

The assurance of God's power at work in history to bring justice was the theological basis for Martin Luther King, Jr.'s call to nonviolent resistance. On June 4, 1957, Dr. King spoke on "The Power of Nonviolence" on the Berkeley campus of the University of California.

> I think every person who believes in nonviolent resistance believes somehow that the universe in some form is on the side of justice. That there is something unfolding in the universe whether one speaks of it as an unconscious process, or whether one speaks of it as some unmoved mover, or whether someone speaks of it as a personal God. There is something in the universe that unfolds for justice and so in Montgomery we felt somehow that as we struggled we had cosmic companionship. And this was one of the things that

kept the people together, the belief that the universe is on the side of justice.

He was reaffirming words he had spoken at the founding of the Southern Christian Leadership Conference earlier that year:

> The method of nonviolence is based on the conviction that the universe is on the side of justice. It is this deep faith in the future that causes the nonviolent resister to accept suffering without retaliation. He knows that in his struggle for justice he has cosmic companionship . . . . Evil may so shape events that Caesar will occupy a palace and Christ a cross, but one day that same Christ will rise up and split history into A.D. and B.C., so that even the life of Caesar must be dated by his name. So in Montgomery we can walk and never get weary, because we know that there will be a great camp meeting in the promised land of freedom and justice.
>
> May all who suffer oppression in this world reject the self-defeating method of retaliatory violence and choose the method that seeks to redeem. Through using this method . . . we will emerge from the bleak and desolate midnight of man's inhumanity to man into the bright daybreak of freedom and justice.

In the background, you can almost hear Julia Ward Howe humming:

> Mine eyes have seen the glory
> of the coming of the Lord;
> He is trampling out the vintage
> where the grapes of wrath are stored;
> He hath loosed the fateful lightning
> of his terrible swift sword;
> His truth is marching on.

In the end, all the people of the world will clap their hands with joy over the destruction of arrogant power.

Singing "Glory! Glory! Hallelujah!" in celebration of God's victory over evil is appropriate, but the focus of the hymn reminds us that it is the celebration of God's victory, not the jingoistic celebration of the victory of nation over nation, race over race, or tribe over tribe. As Dr. King so often reminded his followers:

> The nonviolent resister does not seek to humiliate or defeat the opponent but to win his friendship and understanding . . . . Our aim is not to defeat the white community, not to humiliate the white community, but to win the friendship of all of the persons who had perpetrated this system in the past. The end of violence or the aftermath of violence is bitterness. The aftermath of nonviolence is reconciliation and the creation of a beloved community . . . . The end is reconciliation, the end is redemption.

Nahum saw that "the Lord is slow to anger, but great in power" (Nah. 1:3, *NRSV*). The power of God's judgment is turned against any people, any nation that "plots evil," "counsels wickedness" (1:11), or becomes the adversary of God's vision of peace (1:15). The faithful people who are promised the Lord's protection are not those of a particular race, nation, or clan, but all those who share in God's vision of shalom, the people who can see God's grace at work, even when their own nation experiences God's wrath.

If I had been there, I might have left Nahum out of the canon. It remains a very disturbing warning to a nation enthralled with its military power. But one day, we will clap our hands in joy, in celebration of God's victory over evil.

Seven

A GREAT DAY IN GOTHAM CITY
Zephaniah, Prophet of Reformation

> *The work is great and difficult, but God the*
> *Master of all difficulties is our helper . . . .*
> *the King, the builder of this city . . . hath*
> *opened His mind to His people.*
>
> —*St. Augustine*

MY STUDY OF THE MINOR PROPHETS BEGAN in the
summer of 1989, just as Hollywood was releasing the new
Batman movie. I had been warned that it was a flying leap
from the "Ka-boom" and "Zowee" television series. This was
a serious Batman, waging a serious battle for truth and justice,
a struggle that can be downright gruesome sometimes. But no
one had prepared me for the eerie, pervasive gloom that hangs
over Gotham City throughout the film.

Everything is dark, dirty, drab and gray. The streets are
wet, conveying the feeling of a cold, damp drizzle. The
lighting is dim and artificial, like the light from worn out
florescent tubes. There is not a single ray of sunshine in the
entire film. In all of Gotham City there is not a solitary living

plant; not a tree, shrub, blade of grass, or flower, except for the roses Bruce Wayne lays on the sidewalk where his parents were murdered. The city is shrouded in gloomy darkness, overwhelmed by a sense of weary decay. It could have been a contemporary interpretation of Zephaniah's vision of Jerusalem in 640 B.C.

In contrast to the rural prophets who emerged from the lower classes, Zephaniah was an urban prophet, a man of the city. He was probably a descendant of King Hezekiah of Judah. Almost certainly, he lived "uptown," among people with wealth and power.

Seeing all too clearly the destruction that would inevitably come unless there were major reforms, Zephaniah foresees a day of darkness, a day without sunshine, a day when God's judgment will be poured out on the city he loves. He hears the Lord say,

> I am going to destroy everything on earth, all human beings and animals, birds and fish. I will bring about the downfall of the wicked. I will destroy all mankind and no survivors will be left . . . . The day when the Lord will sit in judgment is near.
>
> —Zephaniah 1:2,7

He warns the people of Jerusalem:

> The great day of the Lord is near—very near and coming fast! . . . It will be a day of fury, a day of trouble and distress, a day of ruin and destruction, a day of darkness and gloom, a black and cloudy day.
>
> —Zephaniah 1:14-15

"Day of the Lord" is the Old Testament formula for the prophetic expectation that one day God would intervene in human history to clean things up and set things right. On that day, God would defeat Israel's enemies, right their wrongs, correct injustice, chastise immorality, and punish those who abused the poor. Then God's righteousness would be fulfilled.

Zephaniah envisions a day of judgment. He pictures the Lord going through the city with lamp in hand, searching out "people who are self-satisfied" and who say to themselves, "The Lord never does anything" (Zeph. 1:10-13). Inevitable judgment falls on people who live and act as if Yahweh no longer governs the world, as if God is no longer present, as if they can run the world by themselves without concern for God's purpose, as if there is no word of justice or judgment for their actions.

Old Testament scholar Elizabeth Achtemeier tells the story of a man in one of the churches she pastored who confessed, "I believe in God, but I don't believe he does anything." Aren't there days when all of us are tempted to say, "I believe in God, all right. I believe that God exists, but I don't believe that God actually does anything. And I certainly don't plan to live as if God were an active presence in my daily experience, as if I thought that God actually might meet me on the street corner."

Several years ago a book review in *The New Yorker* began with these words:

> Even if we cannot believe that God is dead, it is clear that something has died. And that is the capacity of most of us for conducting our daily lives as if He were about, as if His existence and His interest in our affairs were fairly probable.

In the spirit of the prophets, the reviewer went on to say:

> This incapacity may have already had drastic consequences. It may be an honest explanation of the barbarism and confusion that attack our politics, and it may help to account for the turbulence in the private climate of the age.

I have returned to those lines many times because they are such an accurate description of the way so many of us live. They were written for the city folks who read *The New Yorker,* but they could have been written by the city prophet named Zephaniah, who was equally convinced that we experience drastic consequences when we lose the capacity to conduct our daily lives as if we actually believe that God is involved in our affairs. Those lines from *The New Yorker* would have fit quite nicely just above these words from the prophet:

> Jerusalem is doomed, that corrupt, rebellious city that oppresses its own people. It has not listened to the Lord or accepted his discipline. It has not put its trust in the Lord or asked for his help. Its officials are like roaring lions; its judges are like hungry wolves, too greedy to leave a bone until morning. The prophets are irresponsible and treacherous; the priests defile what is sacred, and twist the law of God to their own advantage.
>
> —Zephaniah 3:1-4

In *Batman*, the final struggle between Batman and the Joker, between good and evil, takes place in the church. The two of them climb up into the bell tower of the Gotham City Cathedral which is musty, empty, boarded up, and in utter disarray. It is obviously unused, abandoned, neglected, ignored. As I watched, I couldn't help but think: Zowee! Could the screenwriters be suggesting that the gloom over Gotham City was because the people had abandoned the cathedral, neglected to worship, and given up on God? Could they be suggesting that what happened to Gotham City is what happens to any people when they ignore God, when they become self-satisfied and say to themselves, "The Lord never does anything"? Is this the judgment that falls inevitably upon people who lose the capacity to conduct their daily lives as if God were about, as if God's involvement in their affairs were fairly probable?

I have no illusion that the screenwriters are Old Testament theologians, but whether they realize it or not, the message which spoke to me in the bell tower scene is exactly what Zephaniah had in mind. It is the word of judgment that falls inevitably upon those who choose to live as if God were totally unrelated to their daily lives. It is a day without sunshine, devoid of music, dancing, or joy.

But Zephaniah adds a twist with one small word, a word that I learned to watch out for a long time ago. In Zephaniah 3:5, the prophet says, "But . . . ." Now that word generally indicates a contradiction, a complete reversal, a turning of the tables. One of St. Paul's favorite phrases is "But God . . . ." The apostle piles up all the evil of the world on one side and then says, "But God, who is rich in mercy, out of the great love with which he has loved us even when we were dead through our trespasses, made us alive together with Christ" (Eph. 2:4-5, *NRSV*).

In the same spirit, Zephaniah affirms, "But the Lord is still in the city; he does what is right and never what is wrong. Every morning without fail he brings justice to his people" (Zeph. 3:5).

And the promise comes back to Zephaniah: "Then I will change the people of the nations, and they will pray to me alone, not to other gods. They will all obey me . . . . I will remove everyone who is proud and arrogant, and you will never again rebel against me on my sacred hill. I will leave there a humble and lowly people, who will come to me for help. The people of Israel who survive will do no wrong to anyone, tell no lies, not try to deceive. They will be prosperous and secure, afraid of no one" (Zep. 3:9-13).

The prophecy that begins with a dirge ends with a song of joy:

> Sing and shout for joy, people of Israel.
> Rejoice with all your heart, Jerusalem!
> The Lord has stopped your punishment;
> he has removed all your enemies.
> The Lord, the king of Israel, is with you;
> there is no reason now to be afraid.
> —Zephaniah 3:14-15

In one of the most colorful images of God to come from any of the prophets, Zephaniah pictures Yahweh joining in the celebration.

> The Lord will take delight in you,
> and in his love he will give you new life.
> He will sing and be joyful over you,
> as joyful as people at a festival.
>   —Zephaniah 3:17

The day of doom becomes a day of celebration; the day of judgment becomes a day of forgiveness; the day of darkness becomes a day of light; the day of death becomes a day of new life. On that day, in the language of St. Augustine, the earthly, sinful, rebellious city becomes, by God's power, the eternal city of God.

Let me try to lift this prophecy out of Jerusalem, out of Gotham City, and set it down in the world in which we live.

In our own time, we are called, even as Zephaniah was called, to be God's prophetic people, to proclaim the day of the Lord. By our words, our work, and our worship we bear witness to God's prophetic judgment on every form of evil, injustice, oppression, and sin. We are called to declare that we, like the people of Jerusalem, are doomed when we conduct our daily lives as if God were not about, when we live and act as if we can run the world under our own power.

In every service of baptism we ask the person receiving the sacrament or the parents and sponsors of children, "Do you renounce the spiritual forces of wickedness, reject the evil powers of this world, and repent of your sins?" We ask the congregation, "Do you, as Christ's body, the church, reaffirm both your rejection of sin and your commitment to Christ?" It is our way of declaring God's judgment upon, and our independence from, the destructive forces at work in the human family.

At the same time, we are called to be a prophetic people who announce the good news that God is still in the city. God hasn't given up on us yet. New life and hope are available for those who trust in God.

Jesus said that the day of the Lord is near, so near that you can grasp it in the next breath you take. There are days in our lives when we need to hear God's word of judgment on our self-centered pride, our arrogance, our greed, our insensitivity to the needs of others around us, and our unwillingness to be faithful disciples of Jesus Christ.

There are days when we need to hear God's word of salvation. Days when we desperately need to know that God is still with us, and that God loves us, and that God will give us new life. There are times for each of us when we need to hear someone say:

> Rejoice with all your heart . . .
> The Lord has stopped your punishment
> The Lord, the King of Israel, is with you;
> there is no reason now to be afraid.
> The Lord your God is with you;
> his power gives you victory.
> The Lord has stopped your punishment;
> [so stop punishing yourself!]
> he has removed all your enemies.
> The Lord will take delight in you,
> and in his love he will give you
> new life.
> —Zephaniah 3:15-17

Any day, in any city, can become the "day of the Lord" for us when we hear the Spirit say, "I have ended the threat of doom, and taken away your disgrace"(Zeph. 3:18).

Zephaniah says, "Sing and shout for joy. The great day of the Lord is near—very near and coming fast." It could be today.

Eight

HOW LONG, O LORD?
Habakkuk, Faithful Prophet
of the Long Haul

*With world conditions as they are, there are two
ways in which one can face the situation. He
may say, "Christ's way of life has failed—it is
too soft for a brutal world." Or he may say,
"Everything else has failed except Christ's way
of life—therefore I'll put my trust in God."*
—Dr. Albert Belyea

EVEN IF YOU ARE A CHURCHGOER, the odds are good that
you do not recognize the name of Habakkuk. The odds are
also good that you have never read Habakkuk's prophecy. But
the odds are just as good that somewhere, sometime, you have
asked his questions.

O Lord, how long must I call for help before you listen,
before you save us from violence? Why do you make me
see such trouble? How can you stand to look on such
wrongdoing?

—Habakkuk 1:2-3

Odds are that when you fold up the morning paper or click off the evening news you have been known to sigh:

> Destruction and violence are all around me, and there is fighting and quarreling everywhere. The law is weak and useless, and justice is never done. Evil men get the better of the righteous, and so justice is perverted.
>
> —Habakkuk 1:3-4

There is a disturbing familiarity and timelessness about his complaint:

> How can you stand these treacherous, evil men? . . . Why are you silent while they destroy people who are more righteous than they are?
>
> —Habakkuk 1:13

For Habakkuk, "they" are the Babylonians, the dominant military power of the seventh century B.C. Power was their god (Hab. 1:11).

Habakkuk could see them coming. Having destroyed Nineveh in 612 B.C. and defeated Egypt in 605 B.C., it was only a matter of time until the Babylonians would march across the borders of Judah, clearing the way for the fall of Jerusalem and the exile of the Hebrew people that began in 587 B.C.

He can see them coming, and he cries, "How long, O Lord, before you save us from such violence? How long will you put up with these violent people? How long will evil people get the better of the good folks?"

We still ask those questions. When we experience violence, whether it is the violence of death squads in El Salvador or purse snatchers in Times Square; when we confront injustice, whether it is the raging injustice of apartheid or the injustice of unfair divorce settlement in the local courthouse; when we are invaded, whether the invasion comes by armed force across a line in the sand or by drug-dealing burglars in our own home; whenever we see the Babylonians coming, we, too, are tempted to lose faith, to turn away from God, to chuck religion and try to make it on our own. With the people of Habakkuk's day, we are tempted to abandon the God of the covenant and succumb to the power of the gods who threaten us.

I visited a couple who had not been inside a church in more than a decade, not since the funeral for their teenage son who was killed in a bizarre car accident on his way to a youth group activity. In their pain they had turned away from God, rejected their religious background, and walked away from the institutional church. But healing had come for them. They found their way back to the faith, and are finding there the strength to face both the past and the future.

To some, a decade of separation from God may seem unusual, but that is just about how it was for the people of Judah. And what made the prophets so different is this: rather than turning the prophets away from Yahweh, the brutal realities of the world drove them into the depths of faith and propelled them more powerfully into the arms of God.

Habakkuk prays, "Lord, from the very beginning you are God. You are my God, holy and eternal. Lord, my God and protector" (Hab. 1:12). He continues: "The Lord is in his holy Temple; let everyone on earth be silent in his presence" (Hab. 2:20).

Habakkuk candidly directs his questions to God because he dares to believe that Yahweh was a god of moral character, "holy and eternal." He continues to anticipate the day when God's justice will be accomplished. He believes that justice is the fulfillment of God's purpose for this world; injustice is what happens when God's order is denied.

Sometimes we get that twisted around. Sometimes we think that justice, fairness, and the conviction that evil should be punished and goodness sustained are our ideas and that we must somehow impose them on a reluctant God. The prophets see it exactly the other way. Justice, fairness, the triumph of goodness in human society are parts of God's plan that are thwarted by the violence, greed, and injustice of the human family.

Where do you suppose our anger toward injustice originates? What is the source of that voice within us that says, "This isn't right! It isn't fair"? The prophets knew that our outrage at injustice is born out of an innate sense of the justice of God. The voice within us that cries out against injustice is nothing other than the voice of God.

When justice was perverted during the time of the Old Testament prophets, when goodness was abused, when bad things happened to good people, the prophet, rather than running from God, ran to God. And he ran to God, not pleading or whimpering as if he had to convince God of something God was reluctant to do, but demanding that God get busy accomplishing what he knew God already intended.

> Now do again in our times
> the great deeds you used to do.
> Be merciful, even when you are angry.
> —Habakkuk 3:2

In his authoritative history of the Holocaust, Martin Gilbert records the memories of Levi Shalit, one of the last survivors of the Warsaw ghetto. He described this scene at Dachau on the Day of Atonement, 1944.

> Here stands Warsaw's last rabbi, his face yellow, hairless, wrinkled, his aged body bent; his hands are rocking like reeds in the wind; only the eyes, sparkling stars, look out towards the cold sky above, and his lips, half open, murmur softly.
>
> What does he say now, how does he pray, this last of the rabbis of Warsaw? Does he lovingly accept the pain and suffering, or does he, through the medium of his prayer, conduct a dispute with the Almighty?
>
> . . . No, he does not beg; he does not pray; he demands! He demands his rights, he calls for justice. Why were his

children burnt by the Nazis, why was his wife reduced to ashes? . . . Where . . . is His hearty, divine mercy?

The rabbi expressed the spirit of prophetic prayer, the spirit with which Habakkuk turns to God:

> I will climb my watchtower and wait to see what the Lord will tell me to say and what answer he will give to my complaint.
> —Habakkuk 2:1

The prophet waits, and God's answer comes back:

> The time is coming quickly, and what I show you will come true. It may seem slow in coming, but wait for it; it will certainly take place, and it will not be delayed . . . . Those who are evil will not survive, but those who are righteous will live because they are faithful to God.
> —Habakkuk 2:3-4

The New Revised Standard Version has it:

> For still the vision awaits its time;
> It hastens to the end—it will not lie.
> If it seems slow, wait for it;
> it will surely come, it will not delay.
> Behold, he whose soul is not upright in him shall fail,
> but the righteous shall live by his faith.
> —Habakkuk 2:3-4, *NRSV*

British scholar James Moffatt set the words to rhyme.

> The vision has its own appointed hour;
> it ripens. it will flower;
> if it be long, then wait,
> for it is sure, and it will not be late.

The answer to Habakkuk's question, to your questions and mine, is that God is still at work in this world. The time will come when God's vision for the world will be fulfilled. One day "the earth will be as full of the knowledge of the Lord's glory, as the sea is as full of water" (Hab. 2:14). One day God's kingdom will come, and the will of God will be done on earth as it is in heaven. One day the lion will lie down with the lamb, the swords will be turned into plowshares and the spears into pruning hooks. One day justice will be done, the poor will no longer be oppressed by the rich, and the powerless will no longer be abused by the powerful.

The vision awaits its appointed hour. If it seems slow in coming, keep watching for it and keep working toward it. Continue to be faithful to the vision, living and acting as men and women who know that God is at work with them, even when the fulfillment of the vision seems a long way off.

I, for one, can hardly read these verses from Habakkuk without remembering the way Martin Luther ignited the fires of the Reformation with his rediscovery that "the just shall live by faith." But studying Luther's text in the setting of Habakkuk's prophecy has changed its meaning for me. I understood this text "spiritually," as the description of our relationship with God. Justification is what happens in the soul of the believer who receives God's grace and places his or her faith in Jesus Christ. That is true, based on the way Paul uses this verse in Romans 1:17. But Habakkuk was not describing the justification of the believer through faith in God. He was affirming God's ultimate justification of the world, anticipated and experienced by those who live by faith.

In the rugged realities of a sometimes unjust, violent, and confusing world, the righteous ones live by faith, faith in the God who is still at work in human history, faith that the vision has its appointed hour.

If you look closely, you can see that kind of faith in a person's eyes. In my research on this text, I found a picture of a statue of Habakkuk that is carved into the exterior wall of a cathedral in Genoa, Italy. The prophet is in his watchtower, partially bent at the waist, one hand holding a scroll, the other thumping his chest, asking, "How long, Lord? How long?"

But the eyes, even carved in stone, are like the eyes of that last rabbi from Warsaw: "sparkling stars looking out at the cold sky." They look beyond the immediate circumstances with a steady, concentrated, hopeful gaze, as if the prophet can see something coming, just appearing on the far horizon.

I saw the same "sparkling stars" in the eyes of Walter Sisulu the week after he was released from prison. In 1963, the South African government put him in prison because he dared to call for the justice and freedom which we in America take for granted. For ten years he labored with a pick and shovel in the lime quarry on Robbins Island. It was sixteen years before he was permitted to read the newspaper. At seventy-seven he appeared greyheaded when he was interviewed on the evening news. But I saw that sparkle in his eyes as he described the hard labor, the calloused hands, the long isolation. There was soft-spoken power and decisive strength in his voice when he said, "It's coming. I can see freedom coming. Not right away, but perhaps now, within my lifetime."

The interview ended. There was a moment of silence in the house. My wife said, "Now, that's faith!"

It is precisely that kind of faith that enables Habakkuk to end his prophecy on a joyful note of confidence and praise:

> Even though the fig trees have no fruit
> and no grapes grow on the vines,
> even though the olive crop fails
> and the fields produce no grain,
> even though the sheep all die
> and the cattle stalls are empty,
> I will still be joyful and glad,
> because the Lord God is my savior.
> The Sovereign Lord gives me strength.
> He makes me sure-footed as a deer
> and keeps me safe on the mountains.
> —Habakkuk 3:17-19

We may not be familiar with Habakkuk, but we are familiar with his questions because we have them ourselves. May we also come to affirm his faith.

Nine

BUILD AND HE WILL COME
Haggai, Prophet of Restoration

*God's working shapes reality, and finally his
people must shape their lives to that sovereign
working if they want to live in the real world.*
                                    —*Elizabeth Achtemeier*

A FASCINATING MOVIE captured the attention of American
audiences in 1989. No one expected it to. It had no violence,
no sex, no profanity. There were no guns, no speeding cars,
no fiery explosions—none of the things that usually guarantee
box office success. It was, in fact, a gentle, quiet, mystical sort
of a story, on the edge of sheer fantasy. Some of the critics had
a difficult time explaining why it hooked the hearts and
inspired the imaginations of so many people.

The movie was *Field of Dreams,* based on a 1962 novel by
W.P. Kinsella entitled *Shoeless Joe.* It is the story of an Iowa
corn farmer who, walking through his corn field one summer

evening, hears a barely audible voice whisper, "If you build it, he will come." He tries to ignore the voice, but gazing out across the waving rows of corn, he catches a vision. He knows what he is to build: a baseball stadium. And he knows who will come if he does: Shoeless Joe Jackson. Shoeless Joe Jackson was the left fielder for the 1919 Chicago White Sox, the infamous team that threw the World Series that year, giving us that immortal line, "Say it ain't so, Joe." Shoeless Joe and seven other players were suspended from the game for life. He died in 1951. But three decades later, in the movie, a farmer, who also happens to be a life-long baseball fan, receives the message: "If you build it, he will come."

And so, to the consternation of his neighbors, the amazement of his wife, the frustration of his brother-in-law the banker, and the wonder of his daughter, he builds a baseball field, complete with lights and bleachers, right in the middle of his corn field. It is a costly decision that could mean the loss of the farm, but for those with eyes to see—not the ones who are so nearsighted they cannot see the future, or the ones so tightly focused on things physical that they cannot see things spiritual—Shoeless Joe comes! Shoeless Joe and the whole scandalized team come back and play baseball again. The past is forgiven, the broken relationships are healed, the old dreams are realized, everything is made whole. A writer, brought to Iowa by the farmer to see the whole scene, joyfully pronounces it "Unbelievable!" The farmer replies, "No, it's more than that—it's perfect." Perfect is the same word the New Testament writers use for wholeness, a word not far removed from the Old Testament vision of shalom.

In the final scene of the movie, as the camera pulls away from the field and looks out across the horizon, the viewer gets a long look at an endless line of cars on the highway leading toward the baseball field in the corn field, a twentieth century vision of the promise of Isaiah and Micah:

In the days to come
the mountain where the Temple stands
will be the highest one of all,
towering above all the hills.
Many nations will come streaming to it,
and their people will say,
"Let us go up the hill of the Lord."
—Micah 4:1-2

With that image in your mind, take a running broad jump back to the sixth century before Christ. In 597 B.C., Zephaniah's ominous warnings of invasion were fulfilled and the deportations began, in much the same way the Nazis invaded Poland in 1939 and began deporting Polish Jews to Auschwitz. In 587 B.C., the conquerors sacked Jerusalem, destroyed the Temple, and carried the rest of the people into exile. It lasted until 539 B.C., when Cyrus, the Persian, conquered Babylonia and the first Hebrew refugees were allowed to return home. In 521 B.C., under the leadership of Zerubbabel, a second, larger group returned to rebuild the Temple of Jerusalem.

When the exiles returned to Jerusalem, they discovered that everything had been swept away; the city was completely destroyed. They went to work rebuilding their homes, replanting their farms, and restoring the city, except the Temple, which was left in ruins.

Among them was a man named Haggai. One summer day in 520 B.C., Haggai hears the voice of the Lord asking, "My people, why should you be living in well-built houses while my Temple lies in ruins?" (Hag. 1:4) The voice goes on and he receives this command: "Go up into the hills, get lumber, and rebuild the Temple; then I will be pleased and will be worshiped as I should be" (Hag. 1:8).

With the command came this promise: "I will be with you . . . . I will give my people prosperity and peace" (Hag. 1:13, 2:9).

It sounds like a story about an Iowa farmer hearing a voice say, "If you build it, he will come."

Why was the Temple so important to Haggai? The Temple was the physical symbol of the spiritual presence of God among the people. You could describe it the way Christian tradition describes the sacraments: "an outward and visible sign of an inward and spiritual grace." It was the concrete reminder of God's presence at the center of the nation. The prophets believed that when the Temple was in order, all of life would be rightly-oriented around their identity as the people of God.

So Haggai calls the people to put their lives in order, and to re-orient their common life around their worship of Yahweh. God's word to Zerubbabel, the governor, and Joshua, the High Priest was, "Don't be discouraged, any of you. Do the work, for I am with you" (Hag. 2:4). The message was simple: Get to work. Build a place at the center of your life for God to take up residence. Your painful past will be healed, your shame will be removed, God's vision will be fulfilled, all of life will be right and whole. Build it, and God will come.

Notice that the whole business begins with God. Haggai does not have to rebuild the Temple to convince God to come. Yahweh is not like a reluctant baseball team that won't move to your city unless you build them a new stadium. God is not a first-round draft choice who needs to see a megabuck contract and a Mercedes before signing. There is no question about God's desire to live among us. God takes the initiative. "The Lord inspired everyone to work on the Temple" (Hag. 1:14).

But God will not barge into human life the way the conquering armies came into Jerusalem. The Lord of history does not come crashing in to take control by brute force like the Babylonians. God, who desires shalom for people more than they desire it for themselves, dwells among those who are ready to receive the divine presence, people who order their lives and their world in ways that are consistent with God's purpose.

In the early pages of the Gospel of Luke, we hear the same call from the last person to stand in the line of the great Hebrew prophets, John the Baptist. He appears in the wilderness quoting Isaiah:

> Prepare the way of the Lord,
> make his paths straight.
> Every valley shall be filled,
> and every mountain and hill
> shall be made low,
> and the crooked shall be made straight,
> and the rough ways made smooth;
> and all flesh shall see the salvation of God.
> —Luke 3:4-6, *NRSV*

The prophets consistently offer God's call to repentance: the invitation to acknowledge our sin, to face up to our past, to experience God's forgiveness, and to turn in a new direction, reordering our lives around the expectation of our coming Lord.

The first time Shoeless Joe appears in the Iowa corn farmer's ball field, he asks, "Is this Heaven?" The farmer replies, "It's Iowa." The audiences laugh, the way some may have laughed at Haggai's call to rebuild the Temple, the way the world laughs at the vision of shalom, the way we are tempted to laugh at the idea of God's kingdom coming here, on earth, among us. But that's exactly the point. It is precisely here, in places like Iowa and Orlando, Johannesburg and Capetown, Berlin and Bejing, that the kingdom comes. Ordinary folks like us hear the Spirit say, "Do the work, for I am with you." For people with eyes to see, the vision is already being fulfilled.

I saw it in the witness of the Body of Christ caught in the crucible of suffering in South Africa. It was present in the laughter of children at a preschool program for children from the streets of Johannesburg, in a primitive medical clinic serving the sprawling squatter settlement at Vlakfontein, in the strong, warm laughter of a pastor in the heart of Soweto, in the sparkling eyes of an Anglican priest sentenced to prison for resisting military service, and in the racial diversity of worship of Central Methodist Church. Everywhere I turned I found men and women who had heard the Spirit say, "Do the work, for I am with you." These people dared to believe that if they build it—if they ordered their lives around the vision of the kingdom of God—God will come. The purpose of God will be accomplished. The kingdom will come on earth as it is in heaven.

I returned to my own community with new eyes to see the Kingdom coming among us. I found it in the care that people gave to parents who had lost their only child in an automobile accident, in a group of people sharing the common search for a way to be peacemakers in a nation on the brink of war, in the singing of children in a Sunday School class, in the food line at a homeless shelter, in the building of a house for Habitat for Humanity, in a school teacher's care for an abused child, and in a counseling session with a young couple seeking practical ways to live out their commitment to put God at the center of their marriage and family.

If you have eyes of faith to see, you will find the promise being fulfilled among men and women who are shaping their lives and their world around the vision of shalom, the promise of the kingdom of God.

We, too, are called to complete the work our master began. The word through Haggai is still a living word for us today: "Do not be discouraged. Do the work, for I am with you." Build it, and he will come.

Ten

A PEEK AT THE LAST PAGE
Zechariah, Prophet of the
Triumphant King

We've got some difficult days ahead. But it doesn't matter with me now. Because I've been to the mountaintop. And I don't mind . . . . I just want to do God's will. And He's allowed me to go up to the mountain. And I've looked over. And I've seen the promised land.

—*Martin Luther King, Jr.*

I CONFESS: I AM A COMPULSIVE LAST-PAGE READER. I always sneak a peek at the closing lines of a novel before I finish reading it. Ken Follett's best-seller *The Pillars of the Earth* was the latest. I had barely finished the first chapter when I furtively turned to the last page to read the closing paragraph.

To my surprise, I recognized the scene from college drama and a community theatre production of *Murder In The Cathedral* where I played the leading role of Becket. In the scene, King Henry II is kneeling in repentance at the tomb of Thomas Becket, the murdered archbishop. Follet's last sentence describes the response of Philip, his central character.

"After today," he thought, "the world will never be quite the same."

I still had over nine hundred pages to read. I had no idea what would happen to the characters along the way, but I knew where the story would end.

I am not alone. John Irving, the author of *The World According To Garp* and *A Prayer for Owen Meany,* described the process:

> I wouldn't know how to begin a book if I didn't already know how it ended . . . . I haven't worked out all the seams. But I do know the order of events. And as important as the actual order of events, I know the order in which the events should be revealed to the reader.

John Steinbeck wrote *The Grapes of Wrath* from the perspective of the final page. On Thursday, June 30, 1938, when he finished Book One, he wrote these words in his journal:

> Yesterday . . . I went over the whole of the book in my head—fixed on the last scene, huge and symbolic, toward which the whole story moves. And that was a good thing, for it was a reunderstanding of the dignity of the effort and the mightyness of the theme. I felt very small and inadequate and incapable but I grew again to love the story which is so much greater than I am.

The prophets of Israel read the book of human experience from the perspective of the final page on which they could see the ultimate triumph of God. This eschatological (from the Greek word for "final things") vision of history motivated their calling.

The book of Zechariah, as it is handed down to us, is divided into three distinct sections, written in radically different styles and at very different times. Biblical scholars generally agree that the oracles of "First" Zechariah (chapters 1-8) were written by the prophet described in the Book of

Ezra (Ezra 5, 7). They are clearly dated in 520 and 518 B.C.
(Zech. 7:1). His prophecy contains fantastic visions, many of
which are difficult for the contemporary reader to understand.
His words are addressed to discouraged people who were
facing the massive task of rebuilding their lives in the ruins of
their shattered past. The theme of this first section of
Zechariah is the announcement that the almighty God has
been stirred to action and is moving in history to bring the
exiles home, to restore the nation, and to live among the
people as their ruler and king.

> The Lord said, "Sing for joy, people of Jerusalem! I am
> coming to live among you!" . . .
>
>   He will live among you . . . . Be silent, everyone, in the
> presence of the Lord, for he is coming from his holy
> dwelling place.
>   —Zechariah 2:10-13

Although the exact authorship and date of the later
chapters are difficult to establish with accuracy, some evidence
points toward the end of the fourth century and beginning of
the third century B.C. The second section (chapters 9-11),
reaffirms in poetry the theme of the first section:

> Rejoice, rejoice, people of Zion!
> Shout for joy, you people of Jerusalem!
> Look, your king is coming to you!
> He comes triumphant and victorious,
> but humble and riding on a donkey—
> on a colt, the foal of a donkey.
> The Lord says,
> "I will remove the war chariots from
> Israel and take the horses from Jerusalem;
> the bows used in battle will be destroyed.
> Your king will make peace
> among the nations;
> he will rule from sea to sea."
>   —Zechariah 9:9-10

The third section is written in a more didactic tone, reinforcing the hope of the Lord's triumph, but warning of the struggle and suffering that are a part of the fulfillment of God's rule in human history.

> The day when the Lord will sit in judgment is near. Then Jerusalem will be looted, and the loot will be divided up before your eyes. The Lord will bring all the nations together to make war on Jerusalem . . . . When this will happen is known only to the Lord. Then the Lord will be king over all the earth; everyone will worship him as God and know him by the same name.
>
> —Zechariah 14:1-2, 7-9

An eschatological vision binds the three prophecies together. They proclaim the ultimate triumph of God in human history, even though that triumph will involve conflict between good and evil and involve suffering for God's faithful people. On the last page, all the kings, all the rulers, all the people of the earth will kneel before God, and the world will never be the same again.

It is a great ending, but as I wrestled with it, I began to ask myself, "What difference does it make today? We're not at the end of the story. We are the characters who are tangled up in the chapters of the book. What difference does it make to know how it ends?"

First, this eschatological vision means I don't have to be afraid of history. I know that God's goodness, God's righteousness, God's justice, and God's peace will ultimately triumph.

As I wrote this chapter the President of the United States was sending nearly half a million troops to the Middle East. I was not surprised that that action has given rise to interest in the apocalypse, the end times, the "second coming" as it is called in some Christian circles. A recent headline in *U.S.*

News and World Report asked "Did the Bible Prophesy an Oil War with Iraq?" The opening sentences read:

> The world is headed for apocalypse soon and war with Iraq may be the ignited spark. If one is to believe an increasingly popular refrain among preachers and Bible teachers in some Christian circles, the Persian Gulf crisis is part of a fulfillment of biblical prophecy concerning the end of the world.

There is nothing original about this response to turbulent events. Whenever old empires are collapsing and new empires are emerging, whenever history is shifting its gears, whenever there are times of unrest and change, there are always well-intended people of faith around who will say, "This must be the time. Armageddon is just around the corner, next week at the latest." Their faith may well be motivated by fear that this just might be the end.

Jesus had a very clear response to that kind of fear: "But about that day or hour no one knows, neither the angels in heaven, nor the Son, but only the Father" (Mark 13:32, *NRSV*). He tells his disciples to watch and to be faithful in the work their master has given them to do until the day comes.

In the spring of 1990, months before the Middle East crisis began, William F. Allman wrote:

> In a way . . . Armageddon scenarios contain a grain of truth. The world is a very dangerous place and always has been . . . . Ultimately, the allure of the Apocalypse may lie in the very human trait of wanting simple solutions to complex problems. For some, it might be easier to make the single, big decision to abandon one world for the next than to make the countless, smaller, tougher choices necessary to make this one better.

Many of the people who are fascinated with Armageddon scenarios try to motivate faith on the basis of fear. They talk about how bad the world is, always assuming that someone or something is out to get us. "Everything is going to hell in a handbasket. All we can do is pull the few good folks who are left together and hold on for dear life."

Sometimes it does seem that the world is going to hell, possibly next week at the latest. We are involved in a very real, very difficult struggle for the redemption, the renewal, the constant redirection of our society. It is tough work in which good people do suffer. But as the people of God, we do not act out of fear, but out of faith. We do not live in dread of the devil, but in joyful confidence in our victorious Lord. We know where history is going, and we don't have to be afraid anymore.

And finally, knowing how it ends means this: Right here, right now, we can live under the authority of this God who ultimately will be the triumphant Lord. We do not need to wait for the last page when all the earth will kneel like King Henry kneeling in contrition before Becket's tomb. We can kneel today, offering our lives, our talents, our energy, and our gifts in God's service.

There is a wonderful ordinariness about the closing words of Zechariah:

> At that time even the harness bells of the horses will be inscribed with the words "Dedicated to the Lord." The cooking pots in the Temple will be as sacred as the bowls before the altar. Every cooking pot in Jerusalem and in all Judah will be set apart for use in the worship of the Lord Almighty.
>
> —Zechariah 14:20-21

Even ordinary things—like cooking pots and harness bells—can be dedicated to the Lord. It reminds me of St. Paul telling the Corinthian Christians, "We hold this treasure in earthen vessels—common clay pots—to show that the transcendent glory belongs to God and not to us"(2 Corinthians 4:7, AP). The ordinary work of our lives can be used in the service of the One who will ultimately be recognized as Lord. Here and now, we can know that our lives are dedicated to the larger purpose of the kingdom of God, which one day will be fulfilled on earth.

I love the old story of the man who loved his wife but hated her cat. One day the cat disappeared. The woman was heartbroken. To her surprise, her husband responded with great generosity and offered a $5,000 reward for the return of the cat. Sometime later, when the cat had not been returned, a neighbor asked the man, "Don't you think that $5,000 was a rather extravagant reward?"

The husband replied, "It isn't extravagant if you know what you know."

Sometimes the life of Christian discipleship looks downright extravagant, and by the world's standards, it is. But life takes on a different meaning when you know what you know, when you know that ultimately God's purpose will be fulfilled, that the Lord will be the triumphant king.

Perhaps Christian people are always at their best during difficult times. The Christians in Smyrna faced terrible persecution under Statius Quadratus. Their bishop, the aged Polycarp, was brought to trial. His judge ordered, "You are to renounce the faith. You are to curse the name of Christ!"

But Polycarp gave this answer, "Fourscore and six years have I served Him, and He never did me wrong: How then can I revile my King, my Saviour?" Because he would not renounce his faith, he was burned at the stake. The members of the young church in Smyrna expressed their own defiant faith when they recorded the event: "Polycarp was martyred, Statius Quadratus being proconsul of Asia, and Jesus Christ being King forever!"

Zechariah gives us just a glimpse of the last page, but it is enough for us to know that God will be the triumphant king, and nothing will ever be the same again.

Eleven

WHERE IS GOD'S LOVE?
Malachi, Prophet to
Burned-Out Skeptics

*The Church must ever hold before all people God's
unwavering dream of justice and peace and unity.
Always it must be there on our horizon, calling us
on, no matter what vicissitudes and obstacles on the
journey.*

—*Bishop Peter Storey*

RUSH HOUR IN DOWNTOWN JERUSALEM, 450 B.C.
Chariots are backing up in the streets as business people and
government authorities head for the suburbs. Shop owners are
pulling in their tent flaps. Women gather around the well to
draw water for the evening. Homeless people prepare for
another night on the street. Through the noise of the traffic,
you can hear a loud disturbance. Voices are raised, hands are
waving. Malachi, the "messenger" of God, is at it again,
absorbed in energetic debate like the soap box orators in Hyde
Park, London. People shout their questions. The prophet

turns the inquiry back on the debaters and, before they know it, the accusers have become the defendants.

The proposition is always the same. Malachi declares the words of the Lord: "I have always loved you and I love you still." The questions come back from the crowd: "How have you shown your love for us? Where is the God who is supposed to be just? What's the use of doing what God says?" (Mal. 1:2, 2:17, 3:14, *AP*)

Those are the questions of spiritual depression, the accusations of burned-out skeptics.

Once, the people were excited about their faith. When Yahweh brought them back from exile, they anticipated great things. Certainly the prophetic promises would be fulfilled. They would recover the halcyon days of King David. The land would be miraculously fruitful. All the nations of the earth would come to worship in Jerusalem. The vision, the hope that kept them going through those years of exile would finally be fulfilled.

But sixty years have passed and things haven't turned out the way they expected. Israel is an insignificant speck in the vast Persian Empire, and is ruled by a Persian governor. The land is rocky and unproductive. The economy is in shambles. The Temple has been rebuilt, but worship is a lethargic, careless habit. The offerings are cheap and tawdry. Even the priests ignore the Lord. Deep apathy, weary indifference, and bland skepticism have settled over the people. Over the long haul, their high optimism has worn thin.

I was in South Africa during the days of precarious promise that followed the release of Nelson Mandela. People who had been on the front line of the struggle against apartheid were cautiously optimistic. But within days of my return to the United States, there was news that terrifying violence engulfed the townships around Johannesburg. Innocent men and women were beaten at train stations and roaming gangs destroyed squatter settlements. A South African pastor wrote to me:

The "Beloved Country" is in a great deal of pain and anguish at the moment. Just today we heard of another 30 deaths. This makes us very depressed and heavy-hearted.

A university professor described his spiritual exhaustion:

It has indeed been a time of anguish, with totally mindless killing happening. I have forced myself to try not to respond to the daily roller-coaster of emotion which alternating good and bad news brings . . . . The worst is the exhaustion of spirit which seems often so close. It shouldn't be, of course, but sinful humanity intrudes on God's territory in my soul . . . . I have gone through another bout of pessimism . . . . I feel such confusion because I have always been a positive, optimistic person, seeing in Christian faith the resource to look any problems in the eye and see them as opportunities to give and serve. Now, I do not really know how to handle the unaccustomed heaviness—I do not want to lose the future.

His exhaustion may be similar to the mood of the people with whom Malachi debated. When visions are shattered, when the promise goes unfulfilled, even the most faithful people will ask with the people of Jerusalem: "Where is the God of love? Where is God's justice? What's the use in trying any more?"

So, the debate begins. Malachi counters their questions by pointing to the long story of God's inevitable justice in human history. God's justice may sometimes seem slow in coming, but you can be sure that God's love will not forever endure evil and injustice. For evidence, Malachi reminds his hearers of Jacob and Esau (Gen. 25:24-26). According to tradition, Edom (the people of Esau) had been punished for the violation of the brotherly covenant with Jacob. The fact that they had been pushed off their land by Arab tribes was, for the people of Israel, the evidence of God's judgment against those who oppose God's purpose.

Malachi referred to Jacob and Esau because they were familiar stories to his hearers. The Berlin Wall is more familiar to us. For twenty-eight years it stood as the symbol of political repression. Then, in the fall of 1989, the world watched in amazement as the gates were opened, the barbed wire was removed, and the wall was brought tumbling down. The chunk of the wall that a news correspondent brought back for me bears tangible witness to prophetic faith. Silently, persistently, often unseen and ignored by what we call power in this world, God works for justice in human history.

In his episcopal address to the Synod of the South Western Transvaal District of the Methodist Church, Bishop Peter Storey compared God's work for justice to the flowing tide.

> It is as if God, grown suddenly impatient with our whoring after the false gods of totalitarianism and racial oppression, has dealt history a sudden blow to start huge sections of humanity on a new course, away from madness toward sanity. Certainly in this land, the tide is now flowing irresistibly toward justice. Eddies there may be, with sometimes a contrary wind whipping the surface, but beneath the turbulence the flow is strong and certain . . . .
> We must decide which is the great reality: the contrary wind or the inexorable tide. I place my hope in the tide.

There is, of course, a disturbing side to this principle, particularly if we are on the receiving end of God's judgment. Malachi can see God's love in the way God purifies, refines, and cleanses. God's love will not allow the people of faith to settle for anything less than God's best for their lives and their world. God works through the circumstances of history to purify his people.

Each year during Advent, choirs and orchestras dust off Handel's *Messiah* and again we hear the soloist ask Malachi's probing question:

But who may abide the day of his coming?
And who shall stand when he appears?
For he is like a refiner's fire.

The choir joins in the rousing affirmation:

And he shall purify the sons of Levi
That they may offer unto the Lord
An offering in righteousness.

Handel didn't include the rest of the prophet's message.
The Lord warns:

Then I will draw near to you for judgment; I will be swift
to bear witness against the sorcerers, against the adulterers,
against those who swear falsely, against those who oppress
the hired workers in their wages, the widow and the
orphan, against those who thrust aside the alien, and do not
fear me, says the Lord of hosts.
—Malachi 3:5, *NRSV*

Like Amos and Nahum before him, Malachi describes a
vigorous God whose justice comes as strong soap to cleanse,
whose love comes as refining fire to purify. This God will not
settle for small bargains, but calls us to give the very best that
we have. As the unchanging God of justice and grace, the
Lord calls, "Return to me, and I will return to you."

The only reasonable response from the people is, "How
shall we return?"

Malachi hurls back the shocking rhetorical question,
"Will anyone rob God?" and before the people can respond,
he is into a barn-burning sermon on tithing (Mal. 3:7–10).

This is where the preacher usually loses the congregation.
Mention tithing and some folks go into apoplexy. "Here he
goes," they think, "trying to raise a few extra bucks for the
church. Next thing you know he'll be selling time shares."

In fact, this text has nothing to do with Temple finances
and everything to do with spiritual depression. It has nothing

to do with the church's need for money and everything to do with our need to give. If we want to experience a vibrant, energizing relationship with God, if we want to know the purifying, renewing love of God, we need to give. Generosity is the antidote for spiritual exhaustion. When we shortchange God, we shortchange ourselves.

Malachi reminds the people that the Law said they should bring their best as a tithe to God, and then points out that they were bringing the leftovers. Their carelessness about the quality of their offerings reflected a carelessness about their commitment.

I have never been able to fully explain it, but I have observed that generous people are happy people and stingy folks are grouches. Only when we learn to give generously to God are we ready to experience God's generosity toward us. This is not a game of "Let's Make A Deal" with God. It is not a promise that if I tithe, God will make me rich. The promise is that when we order our priorities around our faith in God, God will make us happy and our land will be a good place to live.

The antidote to spiritual exhaustion for my university professor friend was involvement in the needs of others in the spirit of Christ. In the same letter referred to earlier, he shared his vision for the church to develop new black leadership for South Africa. He told the story of a particular black woman whom he and his wife had enabled, across the years, to become an independent, self-supporting homeowner. He closed the letter by saying,

> I delayed posting this and feel much better already! We may not be able to change the tide dramatically, but there are plenty of opportunities to join with others in the simple and basic task of surviving. That is a privilege . . . . I would certainly still far rather fight for a true faith that stands than see it fade into weakness through lack of exercise. So thank God for difficulties and the promise that in all these things we are more than conquerors.

Malachi closes the debate with a daring challenge: Put God to the test. Just try. Try tithing. Try bringing your whole offering to God. Try being generous in sharing yourself with others, and see if God doesn't open the window in heaven and pour out love and goodness on you.

In the marketplace in Jerusalem, the sun is setting. The streets are deserted, cooking fires fill the air with smoke, today's debate is over. Malachi has turned the tables on them again. For his closing argument, he offers this wonderful picture of God's salvation:

> But for you who obey me, my saving power will rise on you like the sun and bring healing like the sun's rays. You will be as free and happy as calves let out of a stall.
>
> —Malachi 4:2

Where is God's love? You can see it in the way God works for justice in the world. You can see it in the way God refines and purifies faithful followers. You will find it when you learn to give. And then one day, the healing sun will rise on you, and, with Malachi, you will know that God has always loved you and loves you still.

Twelve

WHEN THE LOCUSTS COME
Joel, Prophet of New Dreams

All our salvation begins on the level of common and natural and ordinary things . . . . The coming war, and all the uncertainties and confusions and fears that followed necessarily from that, and all the rest of the violence and injustice that were in the world, had a very important part to play. All these were bound together and fused and vitalized and prepared for the action of grace.

—Thomas Merton

THE FIRST FOLLOWERS OF JESUS were tucked away in an upper room somewhere in the back streets of Jerusalem, perhaps the same room in which they had celebrated the Passover meal with Jesus on the night before his death. They were still reeling from the devastating shock of their master's crucifixion and the revolutionary experience of his resurrection. A surreal atmosphere of sorrow mingled with disbelieving joy must have filled the place. Every dream in which they had invested their lives had been swallowed up by the monstrous fact of Jesus' death.

Herbert Kretzmer caught the spirit of the scene in the Broadway musical *Les Misérables* when Marius, the only survivor of the battle at the barricade, returns to the tavern where he and his young friends had shared their idealistic visions of freedom and justice. He sings:

> There's a grief that can't be spoken
> There's a pain goes on and on
> Empty chairs and empty tables
> Now my friends are dead and gone.
> ....
> From the table in the corner
> They could see a world reborn
> And they rose with voices ringing
> I can hear them now
> the very words that they had sung
> Became their last communion
> On the lonely barricade at dawn.
>
> Oh, my friends, my friends, don't ask me
> What your sacrifice was for.
> Empty chairs at empty tables
> Where my friends will sing no more.

The events of the week following Jesus' death must have had the feeling of a lost campaign, a defeated dream, a shattered hope. Then came the surprise of his resurrection. Suddenly everything was turned on its head. Along with the incomprehensible joy, the narrators record confusion and doubt. They had to have been asking, "Where do we go from here? What does all of this mean?"

The weeks passed. Then came Pentecost, the Jewish harvest festival. The city was packed with faithful pilgrims from around the world. Jesus' followers were gathered in that same upper room when something happened—something so real, so profound that it could neither be denied or explained.

Luke said it was like a strong wind, blowing from heaven and filling the whole place (Acts 2:1-12). It was as if tongues of fire were dancing on their heads. A fiery excitement, a spiritual electricity touched everyone. They were all filled with the Holy Spirit who enabled them to communicate the good news of God's power in Jesus to everyone, each in his or her own native tongue.

When Peter tried to explain what was going on, he reached back across five centuries of tradition to the minor prophets: "This is what was spoken through the prophet Joel" (Acts 2:16-21, *NRSV*).

We know very little about Joel. He was probably a resident of Jerusalem after the rebuilding of the Temple, which would date his prophecy after 515 B.C. His possible references to the rebuilt wall (Joel 2:7, 9) would place him after Nehemiah (440 B.C.), making him the latest of the prophets.

We know that Joel was hurt into poetry by the devastation that came in a plague of locusts. "Swarm after swarm," he reports, "settled on the crops; what one swarm left, the next swarm devoured" (Joel 1:4). The land was stripped bare. Everything was lost. He calls the people to weep over their incalculable loss (Joel 1:4-15).

The prophet was motivated by a specific concern: What will we tell our children? How will we interpret this tragedy to future generations? How is God with us in this devastating experience (Joel 1:1-3)? Peter faced the same task in his Pentecost sermon. What will we say to interpret the death and resurrection of Jesus to the people of Jerusalem? How is God at work in all of this? Sooner or later, every person of faith faces the same task.

Let's acknowledge that difficulties do come to us. People of faith do not have immunity from the devastation. The locusts did not devour the crops of the wicked and bypass the fields of the faithful. Jesus said that the sun shines and the rain falls on good and bad alike (Matt. 5:45). Even when his own time of suffering came, there was no magical escape. No angels protected his back from the whip, no mysterious anesthetic softened the pain. Jesus faced the suffering and death just like everyone else.

The locusts come to all of us. One day each of us will cry "like a girl who mourns the death of the man she was going to marry" (Joel 1:8). The time will come when all of us "look on helpless as our crops are destroyed" (Joel 1:16). It is a universal part of the human experience to face a "dark and gloomy day, a black and cloudy day," and to feel that "there has never been anything like it, and there never will be again" (Joel 2:2).

How will we, how do we, interpret the coming of the locusts in light of our faith? How is God present with us when we face the day of suffering or loss?

For the prophet, the devastation becomes a call to repentance, an opportunity to turn to God in trust and faith.

> Repent sincerely and return to me
> with fasting and weeping and mourning.
> Let your broken heart show your sorrow.
> —Joel 2:12-13

Peter offered the same invitation on Pentecost. When he told the story of the death and resurrection of Jesus, the people were deeply troubled and asked, "What shall we do?"

> Peter said to them, "Each one of you must turn away from his sins and be baptized in the name of Jesus Christ, so that your sins will be forgiven; and you will receive God's gift, the Holy Spirit."
> —Acts 2:38

Whatever else happened in the upper room during those days preceding Pentecost, I am sure the disciples experienced profound soul searching and honest confession as they confronted the awesome reality of the death and resurrection of Jesus. With all defenses down and all barriers broken, they must have shared their brokenhearted sorrow and supported each other in their search for a new future.

Times of loss, grief, or devastation can become times of repentance—times when we acknowledge our inadequacy and turn again to God. They can also become times when we rediscover the mercy of God. The prophet called his people:

> Come back to the Lord your God.
> He is kind and full of mercy;
> he is patient and keeps his promise;
> he is always ready to forgive and not punish.
>   —Joel 2:13

Bishop Woodie White tells of the day he was called from a church meeting to go to his mother's small, humble apartment in the city. Thieves had broken into her house, stolen her possessions, and physically beat her. But he said that when he walked in the door and took her into his arms, out of her long years of faith in the face of suffering, she said to him, "God is good, Woodie. God is still good."

The miracle of faith may not be escape from suffering but rather the discovery of God's grace through our suffering. For those who have nurtured a growing relationship with God, the devastation may be the opportunity to realize anew the constant love (*hesed*) of God that is deeper, stronger, and more long-lasting than our human loss and pain.

Most amazing of all, prophetic faith can see the redemptive power and goodness of God in the midst of life's devastation. Joel hears the Lord saying:

> Fields, don't be afraid,
> but be joyful and glad
> because of all the Lord has done for you.
> Animals, don't be afraid.
> The pastures are green;
> the trees bear their fruit,
> and there are plenty of figs and grapes.

Be glad, people of Zion,
rejoice at what the Lord your God
has done for you."

—Joel 2:21-23

Having told the tragic story of the crucifixion, Peter declares the transforming power of God: "This Jesus whom you crucified, is the one that God has made Lord and Messiah!" (Acts 2:36) God is able to take even the worst act of injustice and sin and use it as the ultimate sign of redemptive love. Even the death on the cross can be transformed into new life in the resurrection.

In 1960, the *Christian Century* magazine asked Martin Luther King, Jr., to reflect on the way his personal suffering had influenced his faith. Dr. King confessed his hesitation because of the danger of developing a martyr complex or appearing to seek sympathy from others, but he wrote the article as a witness to the way personal suffering had shaped his thinking.

> I have been battered by the storms of persecution. I must admit that at times I have . . . been tempted to retreat to a more quiet and serene life. But every time such a temptation appeared, something came to strengthen and sustain my determination.

Dr. King realized that there were two possible responses to suffering: he could react with bitterness or seek to transform the suffering into a creative force. Having chosen the second course, he bore witness to the value of unmerited suffering.

> I have lived these last few years with the conviction that unearned suffering is redemptive . . . . The suffering and agonizing moments through which I have passed over the last few years have also drawn me closer to God.

Prophetic faith discovers the redemptive power of the spirit of God at work through human suffering. The day of devastation can become the day of redemption. Participating in unearned suffering can become a sacrament of God's grace.

Elizabeth Storey has not lived a charmed existence. It has not been easy being married to one of the leaders of the struggle for peace and justice in South Africa.

Elizabeth worked as the Secretary to the General Secretary of the South African Council of Churches. Following the Soweto riots of 1976, the Council provided funds for the burial of children who were killed in the conflict. Elizabeth interviewed the parents who came for assistance to bury their children. They would leave her office infused with a new sense of dignity and some measure of comfort because she had shared their pain.

When I made some naive comment about how hard all this must have been, she smiled and said, "Ah, Jim, we have been privileged to share their pain."

For people of prophetic faith, shared pain can become the redemptive power of God at work in human experience.

This kind of faithful response to the devastation of the locusts results in the gift of a new dream. The promise given to Joel, renewed at Pentecost, was the promise that God's spirit would be poured out on everyone. Don't miss the revolutionary inclusiveness when Joel hears God say, "your sons and daughters will proclaim my message" (Joel 2:28). God promises to pour out the Spirit "even on servants, both men and women" (Joel 2:29). The gift of new dreams for the future will no longer be reserved for those called to be prophets, but will be available to everyone, everywhere. Everyone who responds in faith will be saved.

I spent my last evening in South Africa with Jonathan Cook, a professional psychologist who has invested his adult life in the struggle for justice. Gifted with prophetic vision, he can see in the South African struggle a model of what God might envision for the rest of the world. I still hear him saying, "If we get it right in South Africa, perhaps it will be a model for the rest of the world." He wrote an insightful letter to his professional colleagues around the world in which he concluded:

> We have a land filled with a mixture of so much sadness, so much excitement, so much pain, such wonderfully forgiving sufferers, so much hatred, so much hope, such deep dread, such surprising opportunities. I still feel that out of our experiences could grow wisdom which would be of immense value to the rest of the world . . . . We whites in South Africa could be the pilot study for our distant cousins in the northern hemisphere. We have to learn how to share privilege, wealth and power with a majority which is no longer willing to be kept out . . . . I have sympathy with whites who find this a frightening prospect . . . . But I believe that the same situation will have to be faced on a global scale as the third world majority refuses to continue being kept out. So watch us well, cousins, your turn is next.

Pentecost found the followers of Jesus hiding in fear in the upper room. They were paralyzed, powerless, and paranoid. They had lost everything. But when the Holy Spirit invaded their lives, they were given a new vision of what God intended for their life, their witness, and the world in which they lived. It fulfills the promise which first came to Joel:

> "I will pour out my spirit on everyone;
> your sons and daughters
> will proclaim my message;
> your old men will have dreams,
> and your young men will see visions.
> At that time I will pour out my spirit
> even on servants, both men and women."
> —Joel 2:28-29

The prophets' visions are still being fulfilled: God isn't finished with us yet!

ACKNOWLEDGEMENTS

The scripture quotations not otherwise identified are from the *Good News Bible, The Bible In Today's English,* copyright by American Bible Society 1966, 1971, ©1976, and are used by permission.

Scripture quotations designated NRSV are from the *New Revised Standard Version,* copyright ©1989 by the Division of Christian Education of the National Council of Churches of Christ in the United States of America, and are used by permission.

Scripture quotations designated JB PHILLIPS are from The New Testament in Modern English, copyright ©J.B. Phillips 1958. Used by permission of The MacMillan Company.

Any scripture designated AP is the author's paraphrase.

Excerpts from *Bonhoeffer and South Africa* by John W. de Gruchy. Copyright ©1984 by William Eerdmans Publishing Company. Used by permission of the publisher.

Excerpts from "In Memory of W. B. Yeats" from *W.H. Auden: Collected Poems* by W.H. Auden, edited by Edward Mendelson. Copyright 1940 & renewed 1968 by W.H. Auden. Reprinted by permission of Random House, Inc. and Faber and Faber, Ltd.

Excerpts from *Like It Is!* © by Helen Kromer. Reprinted with permission by Baker's Plays, Boston, MA 02111.

"Epilogue" (Finale) from the musical LES MISERABLES by Alain Boublil and Claude-Michel Schonberg. Music by Claude-Michel Schonberg. Lyrics by Alain Boublil, Jean-Marc Natel and Herbert Kretzmer. ©Alain Boublil Music Ltd. (ASCAP)

Excerpts from *A Testament of Hope: the Essential Writings of Martin Luther King, Jr.* Copyright ©1986 by Coretta Scott King. Reprinted by permission of Joan Daves Agency.

Excerpts from *The United Methodist Hymnal* Baptismal Covenant I, ©1976, 1980, 1985, 1989 The United Methodist Publishing House. Used by permission.

"Empty Chairs At Empty Tables" from the musical LES MISERABLES by Alain Boublil and Claude-Michel Schonberg. Music by Claude-Michel Schonberg. Lyrics by Alain Boublil, Herbert Kretzmer. ©Alain Boublil Music Ltd. (ASCAP)

JAMES A. HARNISH is the pastor of St. Luke's United Methodist Church at Windemere in Orlando, Florida, a congregation he helped to organize in 1979. He has also served other churches in Florida and is actively involved in the civic and religious lives of the community. He and his wife Marsha are the parents of two daughters, Carrie Lynn and Deborah Jeanne.

His previous books include *Jesus Makes the Difference!*, *What Will You Do With King Jesus?* and *Journeys With the People of Genesis*.